This publication was designed for Pre-adolescent Children (9 to 11 years old)

**STUDENT ACTIVITY WORKSHEETS
YEAR 1**

Corresponds to Year 1 of the cycle of three years of WORDS OF LIFE (Pre-adolescent Children) lesson books.

Words of Life (Pre-adolescent Children), Year 1 - Student Activity Worksheets

Published by:

Mesoamerica Region Discipleship Ministries

www.SdmiResources.mesoamericaregion.org

Copyright © 2017 - All rights reserved

ISBN: 978-1-63580-080-7

Reproduction of this material is permitted only for local church use.

All of the scripture verses quoted are from the NIV Bible unless otherwise stated.

Translated into English from Spanish by:

Bethany Cyr, Monte Cyr, Amanda Englishbee (Lessons 1-10, 41-52), Emily Raquel Gularte Oliva (11-30, 33-40), Nancy Mong (31-32)

Printed in the United States

TABLE OF CONTENTS

UNIT I: WOMEN OF FAITH 05
Lesson 1-3

UNIT II: HOW TO MAKE GOOD DECISIONS 17
Lesson 4-8

UNIT III: WHO ARE GOD'S PEOPLE 37
Lesson 9-11

UNIT IV: JESUS, OUR KING 49
Lesson 12-17

UNIT V: THE BIRTH OF THE CHURCH 73
Lesson 18-21

UNIT VI: OUR MISSION: TO REACH OTHERS 89
Lesson 22-25

UNIT VII: PARABLES OF JESUS 105
Lesson 26-30

UNIT VIII: JESUS TEACHES ABOUT PRAYER 125
Lesson 31-34

UNIT IX: SEARCHING FOR TRUE WISDOM 141
Lesson 35-39

UNIT X: ATTITUDES THAT JESUS TAUGHT 161
Lesson 40-43

UNIT XI: ELIJAH: A COMPASSIONATE MAN 177
Lesson 44–47

UNIT XII: CHRISTMAS ACCORDING TO 193
Lesson 48-52

Lesson 1 — Student Workbook

MARTHA DECLARES HER FAITH IN CHRIST

Memory Verse: *"Yes, Lord," she replied, "I believe that you are the Messiah, the Son of God, who is to come into the world."* (John 11:27)

TRUST

What does "trust" mean?
_____
_____
_____
_____
_____
_____

Whom do you trust?
_____
_____
_____
_____
_____
_____

Unscramble the letters of the following words. They will show you when you need to trust in others:

NELLYO

DSA

FIDARA

Think of a time when you needed to trust in someone. Write a word expressing that on the line below the circles. Now, draw in the blank circles a face that expresses those feelings.

People can disappoint us, but we can always trust in ___ ___ ___.

NOTHING IS IMPOSSIBLE FOR HIM

Lazarus sisters were confused and dazed; when he died, they said, "If Jesus would have been here, this would not have happened." Meanwhile, Jesus said to his disciples,

Jesus: Our friend Lazarus has fallen asleep, but I am going there to wake him up.

Disciples: Lord, if he sleeps, he will get better.

Narrator: Jesus said this about Lazarus' death, but they thought he was talking about natural sleep. Then Jesus clearly said, "Lazarus is dead."

Four days later, after Lazarus was buried, the news came that Jesus was coming to the city. When Martha heard this, she went to meet him. She didn't understand why he didn't come any sooner. Didn't Jesus know that they needed his help?

(Jesus approaches and Martha meets him exclaiming,)

Martha: Lord, if you had been here, my brother would not have died. But I know that even now God will give you whatever you ask.

Jesus: Your brother will rise again.

Martha: I know he will rise again in the resurrection at the last day.

Jesus: I am the resurrection and the life. The one who believes in me will live, even though they die; and whoever lives by believing in me will never die. Do you

Martha: (Say to the messengers): You have to find Jesus! He is the only one that can help Lazarus. When you find him, tell him, "Lord, the one you love is sick." He will know what to do.

Narrator: The messengers took the news to Jesus, and came back with an important answer:

Messenger: Jesus said that this disease is not deadly, but for the glory of God, so that the son of God may be glorified by it.

Narrator: Now Jesus loved Martha and her sister and Lazarus. So although he heard that Lazarus was sick, he stayed where he was two more days.

Martha: Where is Jesus? Why didn't he come? He knows that Lazarus is sick. I hope he comes soon. It hurts me to see my brother suffer.

Narrator: But Jesus didn't come.

believe this?

Martha: Yes, Lord, I believe that you are the Messiah, the Son of God, who is to come into the world.

Narrator: She returned to her house and told her sister Mary that Jesus was in town and wanted to see her; and when Jesus saw how Mary and the Jews with her were weeping because of Lazarus' death, he was deeply moved in spirit and troubled. He asked,

Jesus: Where have you laid him?

Narrator: When they showed Jesus the tomb, he wept. Then the Jews said,

Jews: See how he loved him!

Some Other Jews: Could not he who opened the eyes of the blind man have kept this man from dying?

Narrator: Then Jesus went to the grave and said,

Jesus: Take away the stone.

Martha: But, Lord, by this time there is a bad odor, for he has been there four days.

Jesus: Did I not tell you that if you believe, you will see the glory of God?

Narrator: When they removed the stone from the grave, Jesus looked up and said,

Jesus: Father, I thank you that you have heard me. I know that you always hear me, but I said this for the benefit of the people standing here, that they may believe that you sent me.

Narrator: When he had said this, Jesus called in a loud voice,

Jesus: Lazarus, come out!

Narrator: The dead man came out, his hands and feet wrapped with strips of linen, and a cloth around his face.

Jesus: (walks towards some people and says,) Take off the grave clothes and let him go.

TRUST OR DISTRUST

In what situations is it easy to trust Jesus?

_____
_____
_____
_____

In what situations is it difficult or hard to trust Jesus?

_____
_____
_____
_____
_____

In which of these situations is it more difficult for you to trust in Jesus? Put a star next to the situations that are most difficult for you to trust Jesus.

Ask God to help you trust him in the difficult situations. Then give your worries to Him.

Lesson 2

STUDENT WORKBOOK

PRISCILLA TESTIFIES OF HER FAITH

Memory Verse: *"Yes, Lord," she replied, "I believe that you are the Messiah, the Son of God, who is to come into the world."* (John 11:27)

TENTMAKERS TESTIFY ABOUT CHRIST

Priscilla and her husband Aquilla lived in the city of Ephesus, and they made tents. They also happened to be great friends with Paul, and he also made tents when he wasn't too busy with his missionary work.

They were Jews who knew and believed in Jesus Christ as their personal savior, and they all wanted others to know Him too. One day they heard that a man name Apollos was preaching at their local synagogue. They went to hear him speak; he knew a lot about John the Baptist and his disciples, and he told stories from the Old Testament with clarity and preciseness. He taught them that the Savior would come someday.

Priscilla loved to hear him speak, even though Apollos didn't know much about Jesus.

After Priscilla and Aquilla had heard him preach, they invited him to their house and taught him everything they knew about Jesus. They told him that Jesus died on the cross for the sins of the world, and three days after his death he rose again.

Apollos was a good student. He was anxious to tell the other disciples of John the Baptist what he had learned. Afterwards he traveled to many places to share the Good News.

Priscilla and Aquilla continued making tents, but they also opened their home to teach others about their faith in Jesus Christ. This began one of the first early churches. They were happy to be able to teach Apollo about Jesus.

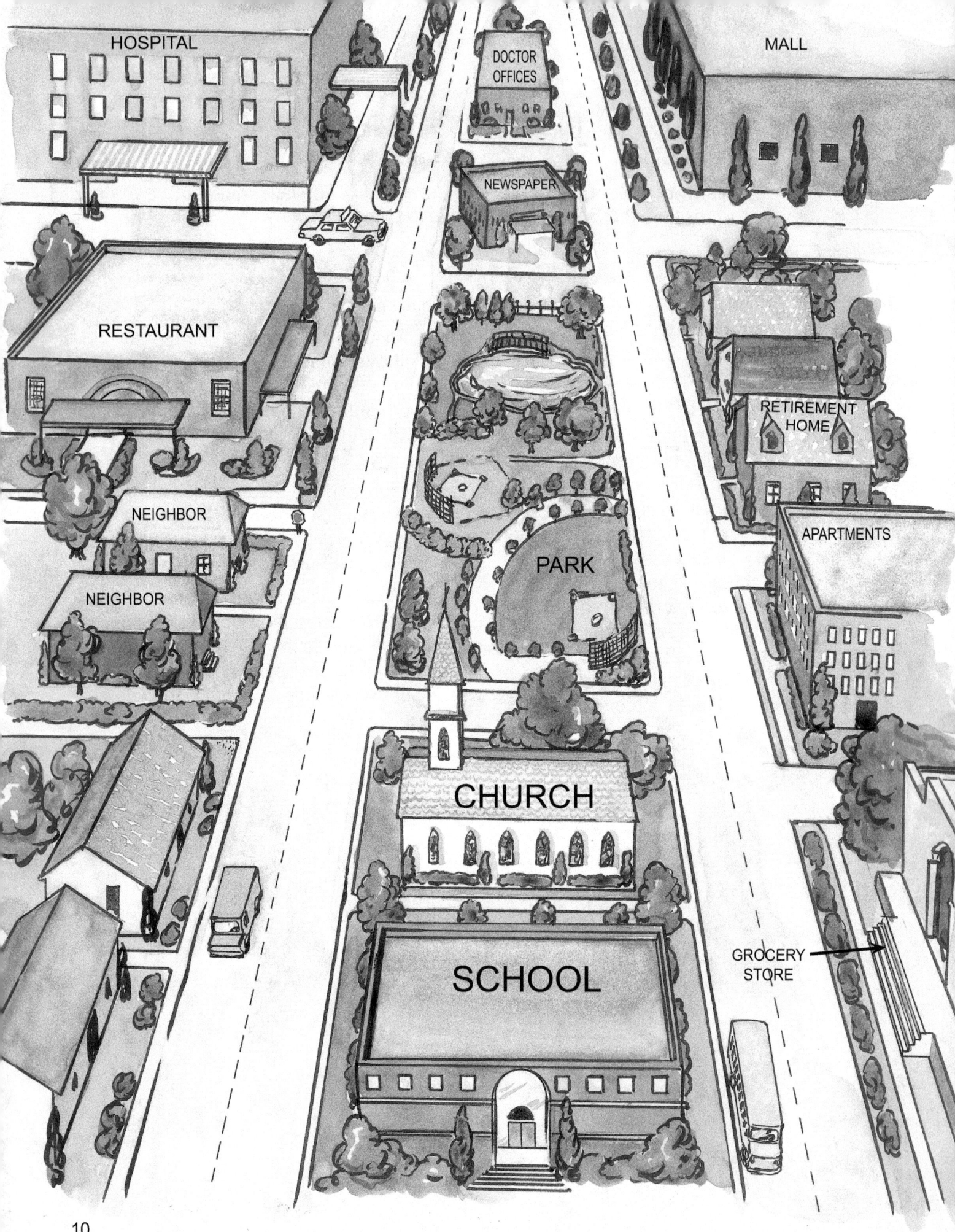

DO YOU KNOW THEM?

Look at the drawing of the town and think about all the people you see every day. Write down the names of the people you know. If you don't know their names, write down what they do or where they work. Put a star next to the ones who have told you that they are Christians and pray for those on your list who are not Christians.

_____ _____
_____ _____
_____ _____
_____ _____
_____ _____
_____ _____
_____ _____
_____ _____
_____ _____

What will you do so that Jesus is not a secret?

Ways you can talk about Christ to people who are not Christians.

1. Invite a friend to watch a Christian movie with you.
2. Listen to Christian music
3. Hang up Christian posters in your room.
4. Read Bible stories to little kids.
5. Give your testimony at church.
6. Pray before you eat.
7. Read Christian books and magazines.
8. Wear shirts that have a Christian theme.
9. Love God and others as yourself.

ACCEPT THE CHALLENGE

Think about the people you know who don't know Jesus as their Savior. Make a list of the ways you can tell them about the love and truth of Jesus.

_____
_____
_____
_____
_____
_____
_____

Now, elaborate on your plan. What will you do?

_____
_____
_____
_____
_____
_____
_____
_____
_____

Prepare to share in the next class about the success you had in speaking to someone about Jesus!

Lesson 3

STUDENT WORKBOOK

LYDIA, A WOMAN OF FAITH IN ACTION

Memory Verse: *"Yes, Lord," she replied, "I believe that you are the Messiah, the Son of God, who is to come into the world."* (John 11:27)

I'll Tell Them

Who do you love very much?

Do you have a special friend that you tell your secrets to? Who is it?

When you're excited or happy, whom do you tell?

Inside the heart, write the names of your friends and family members who are special in your life.

13

Lydia's Wise Decision

There was a woman named Lydia who lived in Philippi. She dedicated her life to selling a very special kind of fabric that was purple.

One of Paul's friends said, "There is no synagogue here and it's the day of rest. Where should we praise and worship God?" Paul answered, "In cities that don't have a synagogue, the people go to the river to praise Him. Perhaps we could find one near here to worship."

They all left the city and went to the shore of the river to join with other Jews to praise God. They hoped to teach them the truths about Jesus, the Messiah that all the Jews waited patiently on who had already come and gone.

"There! There is a group; it looks like we came to the perfect place!" said one of Paul's disciples.

Paul and his friends sat near a group of women; they wanted to hear what Paul and his friends said. One of them was Lydia, a business woman from the city of Thyatira (she sold very expensive purple cloth). Lydia and her friends listened to Paul's words while he told about how Jesus came to earth and died on the cross. Also, how God resurrected him on the third day.

Lydia thought about it. "It's possible that the Messiah has already come! It's everything I have been hoping for forever! I believe in Jesus! Can I be baptized? Also, I want my friends and my family to know about Him." When her family heard the message, they also believed and they were baptized.

Lydia didn't want Paul and his friends to leave because she wanted to know more about Jesus Christ. So, they stayed for quite a while at Lydia's house.

DO YOU KNOW MY FRIEND?

Cut along the solid black lines. Fold in half along the dotted line to form a booklet with 8 pages. Staple the booklet on the fold. Write the corresponding verses in the box of each illustration of Jesus' life.

My friend Jesus wants to be your friend too. He went up to Heaven, but he's also wants to be in your life. He can forgive you for all of the bad things you've done. If you believe in him and repent of your sins, he will forgive you and make you a child of God.

(Acts 1:9-11)

My friend Jesus died on the cross because there were people who didn't like him. He knew that he had to die to pay the ultimate price for our sins. He did it because He loves us so much.

(Mark 15:25-26)

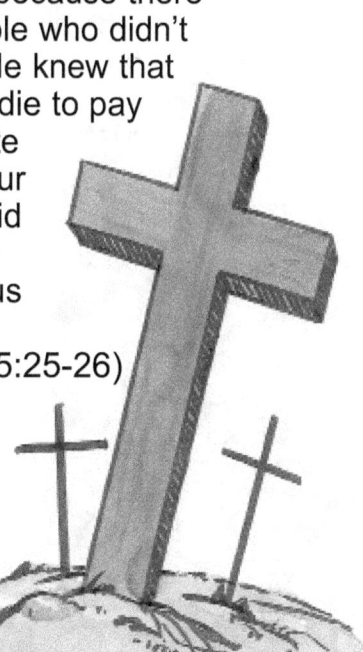

God became man and was born as a baby. He grew up and was an obedient child of God and His earthly parents.

(Luke 2:40)

Do you celebrate Christmas? If you do, you are celebrating my friend Jesus' birthday!

(Luke 2:7)

But, my friend Jesus, even though He was dead, was resurrected on the third day. He conquered death and sin! He lives forever!

(Luke 24:6)

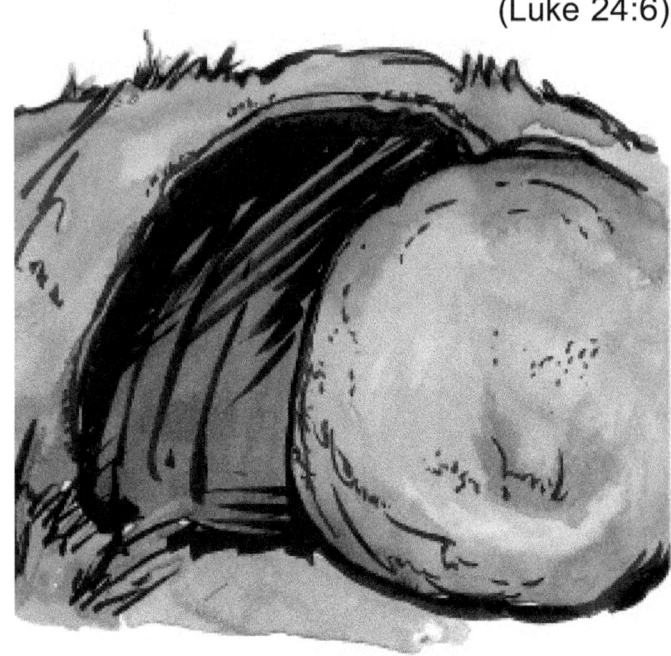

My friend Jesus taught people to love God; He healed the sick, fed the hungry and brought the dead back to life.

(Matthew 5:1-2)

Lesson 4

STUDENT WORKBOOK

TAKE RESPONSIBILITY FOR YOUR DECISIONS!

Memory Verse: "So whether you eat or drink or whatever you do, do it all for the glory of God." (1 Corinthians 10:31)

Which Apple Looks Better?

What looks better may not be what it seems!

Draw a star under the apple you think is the best. Fold the page up along the dotted line.

17

LOT'S DECISION

What looks better may not be what it seems!

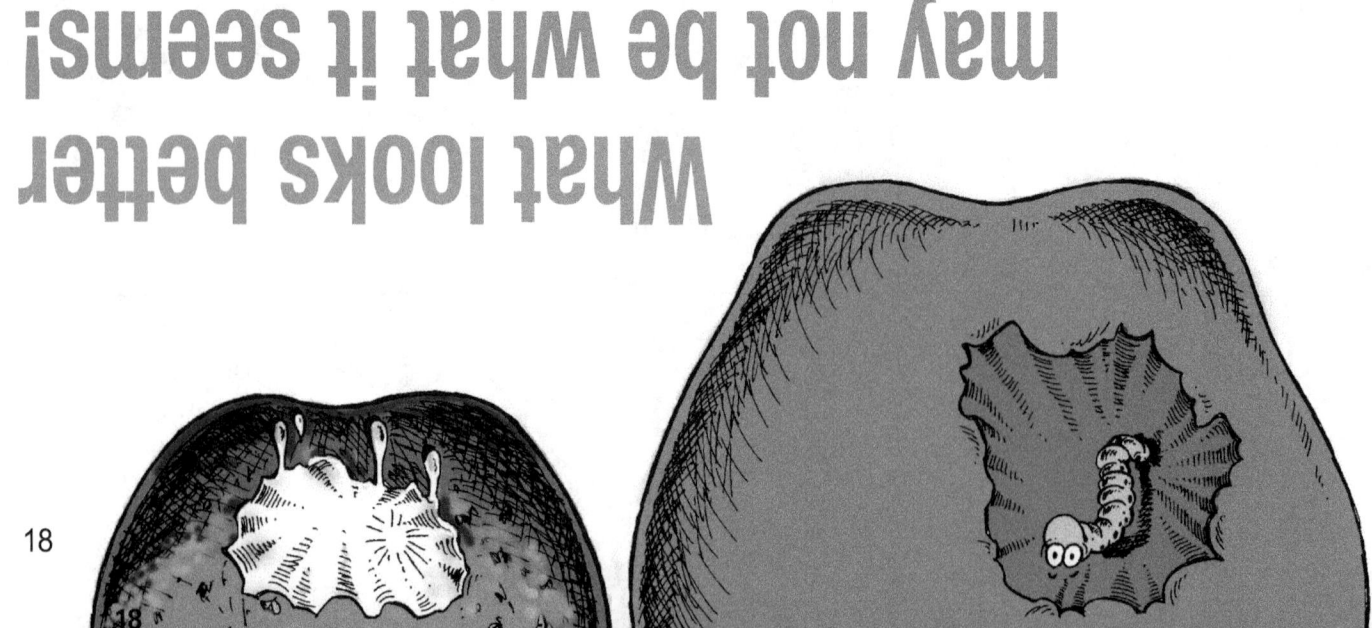

(Lot runs into the tent to find Abraham.)

Lot: Uncle Abraham! Uncle Abraham! Our shepherds are fighting again! (Lot runs into the shop where Abraham was working.)

Abraham: Fighting over pastures again?

Lot: Isn't that what it's always about?! Your shepherds are saying there's not enough grass for your herds AND mine. They won't let my sheep or cows eat here. What are we going to do to solve this problem?

Narrator: Abraham thought for a moment. He owned a lot of sheep and cows, but so did his nephew Lot. And there wasn't enough grass and water for all of the animals if they wanted to stay together. And since he loved Lot, he didn't want to fight with him, so he said,

Abraham: "Let's not have any quarreling between you and me, or between your herders and mine, for we are close relatives. Is not the whole land before us? Let's part company. If you go to the left, I'll go to the right, if you go to the right, I'll go to the left."

Lot: Wow! Abraham is letting me choose which area I want. Even though He is older and my uncle, and he has the right to choose, he is letting me decide. This is great!

Narrator: He looked around and saw the whole plain of the Jordan. It had lots of water, like the garden of the Lord. But there was still a problem – the people who lived in the cities in the valley were evil and perverse. But there's so much grass and water . . . Then Lot chose for himself the whole plain of the Jordan.

Abraham: All right, you go and live in the valley. I'll go to the hills.

Narrator: The two men parted company. Abraham stayed in the land of Canaan, while Lot lived in the cities in the valley. Years later, Lot's herds of sheep and cattle had grown a lot because they had eaten well on the grass of the lowlands. So, Lot became very rich and didn't want to live in tents anymore. He decided to move to the city of Sodom. But the inhabitants of Sodom were evil and they committed horrible sins against Jehovah. Their wickedness was so terrible that God decided to destroy the city. But since Lot was Abraham's nephew, God sent two angels to rescue him and his family.

Angels: Lot, we are going to destroy this place because the evil of the people of this city has gone up before Jehovah. Therefore, Jehovah is going to destroy it. Go and tell your family what is about to happen.

Narrator: Lot spoke to his sons-in-law, the husbands of his daughters, and said,

Lot: Get up, get out of this place, because Jehovah is going to destroy this city.

Narrator: But his sons-in-law thought he was joking. The angels hurried to Lot saying,

Angels: Get up, take your wife and your two daughters so that they don't perish in the punishment of the city.

Narrator: Because Lot delayed, the angels seized his hands, his wife and his two daughters, because of Jehovah's mercy towards them. The angels took Lot and his family out of the city. And when they got away from the city, they told Lot,

Angels: Flee for your lives; Don't look back or stop anywhere in the valley.

Narrator: When Lot and his family were safe, the Lord rained sulfur and fire on Sodom and Gomorrah from the heavens ... then Lot's wife looked back behind her and became a pillar of salt.

(This Bible story is found in Genesis 13:6-13, 19:14-17, 19, 24 and 26.)

DECISIONS!

God has given us all the privilege and responsibility to make decisions. What are some of the decisions that you make?

_____
_____
_____
_____
_____
_____
_____

Put an X next to the decisions that are difficult to make.

What do children your age think about when they make decisions?

_____
_____
_____
_____
_____
_____
_____

What should you think about when you make decisions?

_____
_____
_____
_____
_____
_____

How can you tell if a decision will result in good or bad consequences?

_____
_____
_____
_____
_____
_____
_____

Lesson 5
Student Workbook

USE YOUR TALENTS FOR GOD!

Memory Verse: "So whether you eat or drink or whatever you do, do it all for the glory of God." (1 Corinthians 10:31)

What Are Your Talents?

Each balloon has a different activity written on it. Draw a star on each one that you know how to do well.

WHAT ELSE CAN YOU DO?

_____ _____
_____ _____
_____ _____
_____ _____

Building the TABERNACLE

"Bezalel! Bezalel!" called Oholiab "Where are you off to so fast?"

"I'm going to Moses' tent," responded Bezalel. "He wants to talk with me."

"He asked me to come as well," said Oholiab.

"I wonder what he wants to tell us? I'm sure it has something to do with building the tabernacle," said Bezalel while they hurried to meet Moses.

They knew that God had given plans to Moses to build the tabernacle. This would be a place for the whole city to unite and praise God. Moses told Bezalel and Oholiab that God had chosen them to lead the construction of the tabernacle. This would be a huge mobile tent, since the Israelites traveled so much. Therefore, the tabernacle would look like a tent on the outside but would be amazingly beautiful on the inside.

When Bezalel and Oholiab got to Moses' tent, he greeted them.

"Welcome! I've asked you to come so I can tell you what God told me when I was on Mount Sinai," Moses said. "The Lord said to me, 'Tell the Israelites to bring me an offering. You are to receive the offering for me from everyone whose heart prompts them to give. Then have them make a sanctuary for me, and I'll dwell among them. Make this tabernacle and all its furnishings exactly like the pattern I'll show you.' God has promised that if we do everything exactly as He has instructed us that His presence will descend upon the tabernacle and He will dwell there," continued Moses.

"The city has brought many offerings," said Bezalel.

"Yes," agreed Moses, "we have all the materials that we need.

The city was very happy to give what they had for the construction of the tabernacle.

"They've brought, gold, silver, wood, and fine linen," said Oholiab.

"Now we are ready to get started on building the Tabernacle, just like God showed us," continued Moses.

"What would you like us to do?" Bezalel asked.

"When I was on Mount Sinai," responded Moses, "the Lord also told me, 'See, I have chosen Bezalel son of Uri, the son of Hur, of the tribe of Judah, and I have filled him with the Spirit of God, with wisdom, with understanding, with knowledge and with all kinds of skills—to make artistic designs for work in gold, silver and bronze, to cut and set stones, to work in wood, and to engage in all kinds of crafts. Moreover, I have appointed Oholiab son of Ahisamak, of the tribe of Dan, to help him.'"

Bezalel and Oholiab were happy to have been chosen by God for this job, but they were scared.

When he noticed this, Moses said, "Don't be afraid, God has chosen you for this construction, and he's given you the talents and ability to do so."

"This is such a huge job," said Oholiab, "can we really do it?"

"Yes," replied Moses. "God and the people will help you so you know what to do."

Some artists worked on the wood. Others made decorations out of gold and silver for the inside of the tabernacle. Some sewed animal skins together for the outside of the sanctuary. Others made curtains and still others made clothes for the priests.

(This story is found in Exodus 25 and 31.)

I'll Do It For
GOD

From the "What Are Your Talents" worksheet, choose two of your talents that you will use for God this week and note them on the lines below. Then describe how you will use them for God this week.

Talent	How will I use this talent?
_____	_____
	_____
	_____
	_____
	_____

Talent	How will I use this talent?
_____	_____
	_____
	_____
	_____
	_____
	_____

Next week, be prepared to share with your class how you used your talents for God.

Lesson 6 – Student Workbook

!STOP! BEWARE OF BAD DECISIONS

Memory Verse: "So whether you eat or drink or whatever you do, do it all for the glory of God." (1 Corinthians 10:31)

What Are The Consequences Of...

SMOKING

NOT SMOKING

EXERCISING

NOT EXERCISING

STUDYING

NOT STUDYING

The Truth Is:
Making bad decisions results in bad consequences.
Good decisions are the only decisions that bring good consequences.

"If only I were king," thought Absalom, son of King David. Absalom was very proud of his good looks.

He wanted to take his father's place as king; he got up in the morning and stood on the side of the road, next to the palace door, and asked everyone who came to appear before the king, "What town are you from?" And they would respond, "Your servant is from one of the tribes of Israel." Absalom would then respond, "Look, your claims are valid and proper, but there is no representative of the king to hear you." And Absalom would add, "If only I were appointed judge in the land! Then everyone who has a complaint or case could come to me and I would see that they receive justice."

One day, Absalom asked David's permission to go to Hebron to worship the Lord and David let him go. But in reality, Absalom didn't want to go worship. He wanted to build a palace there, because then he would be king of Israel in place of his father.

As soon as he left, secret messengers were sent throughout the tribes of Israel to say, "As soon as you hear the sound of the trumpets, say, 'Absalom is king in Hebron.'"

Absalom asked Ahithophel, one of David's counselors, to help him take the throne from his father. One day, a messenger came to David and told him, "The hearts of the people of Israel are with Absalom." So David said to all his officials who were with him in Jerusalem, "Come! We must flee, or none of us will escape from Absalom. We must leave immediately, or he will move quickly to overtake us and bring ruin on us and put the city to the sword."

But David continued up the Mount of Olives, weeping as he went. David had been told that Ahithophel was among the conspirators, so he prayed, "Lord, turn Ahithophel's counsel into foolishness."

Hushai was one of the loyal counselors of David. David told Hushai to return to Jerusalem and pretend that he was with Absalom. At first, Absalom was suspicious of him, but Hushai said, "Your Majesty, I'll be your servant. I was your father's servant in the past, but now I'll be

DECISIONS HAVE CONSEQUENCES

your servant."

Absalom wanted to make sure that his father couldn't conquer his kingdom again, so he asked for advice from Ahithophel. Ahithophel told him, "I would choose 12,000 men and set out tonight in pursuit of David. I would attack him while he is weary and weak."

Absalom also asked Hushai what he should do. Hushai knew that Ahithophel's advice would bring bad results for David, and that David and his men needed time to rest and plan their next move. Hushai told Absalom that he should wait until he could get together more men for his army.

So, Absalom and all of Israel said, "The advice of Hushai the Arkite is better than that of Ahithophel."

When Absalom's army finally set out to fight David, David and his men were rested and ready for battle. "King David commanded Joab, Abishai and Ittai, 'Be gentle with the young man Absalom for my sake.' " David's army marched out of the city to fight Israel, the battle took place in the forest of Ephraim.

Now Absalom happened to meet David's men. He was riding his mule, and as the mule went under the thick branches of a large oak, Absalom's hair got caught in the tree. He was left hanging in midair, while the mule he was riding kept on going.

When one of the men saw what had happened, he told Joab, "I just saw Absalom hanging in an oak tree."

Then Joab, David's commander, took three javelins in his hand and plunged them into Absalom's heart while Absalom was still alive in the oak tree. When David heard of his son's death he wept and said, "O my son Absalom! My son, my son Absalom!" David returned to his throne in Jerusalem very saddened.

(This Bible Story is found in 2 Samuel 15:1-37; 16:15-23; 17:1-14, 18:1-33.)

How Do I Make Good Decisions?

Read Proverbs 8:10-11 and fill in the blank spaces.

Choose my _____ instead of silver, _____ rather than choice gold, for _____ is more precious than rubies, and nothing you desire can compare with her.

In other words:
_____
_____
_____
_____

If you're not sure what decision you should make, see what the Bible says about it. Be careful with the decisions you make this week, and be ready to tell others how you have tried to serve God.

Lesson 7 — Student Workbook

DO THE RIGHT THING AND YOU WILL BE DIFFERENT

Memory Verse: "So whether you eat or drink or whatever you do, do it all for the glory of God." (1 Corinthians 10:31)

There is a message hidden in the maze below. Look at it carefully. Start with the letter E and follow the path. Write the letters, as you come to them, on the lines below. Stop when you think you know the phrase and put an X where you stopped.

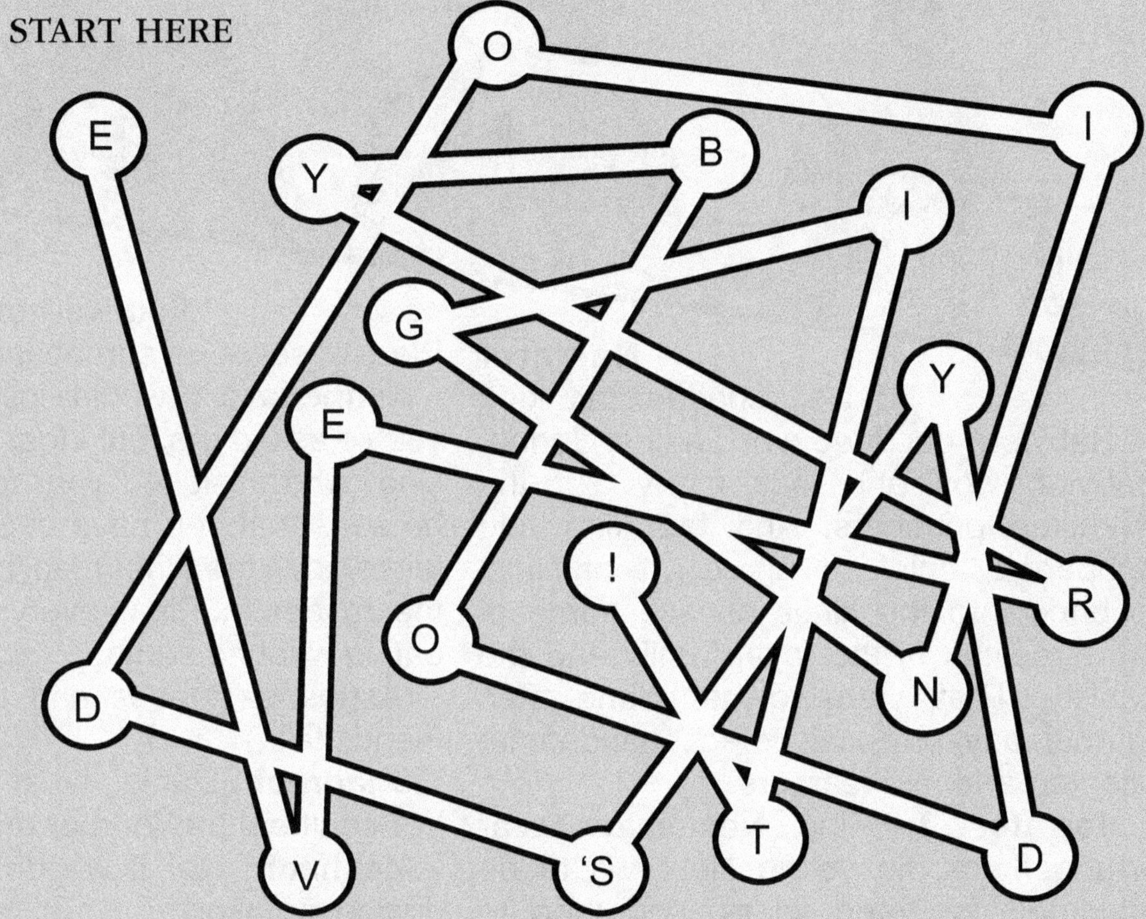

START HERE

___ ___ ___ ___ ___ ___ ___ ___ ___

___ ___ ___ ___ ___ ___ ___ ___

FOLLOW THE LEADER

WE WON'T EAT THAT!

Narrator 1: Nebuchadnezzar, king of Babylon, declared war against Judah. Babylon won and took many of the Israelites prisoners. And the king told Ashpenaz, chief of his court officials, to bring into the kings service some of the Israelites of the royal family and the nobility. They were to be young men without any physical defect, handsome, talented and fast learners.

Narrator 2: King Nebuchadnezzar arranged for the young Hebrews to be educated for three years, and then to appear before him. Among the young prisoners were Daniel and his three friends, Hananiah (Shadrach), Mishael (Meshach) and Azariah (Abednego).

Ashpenaz: (directing himself towards Daniel and his friends) King Nebuchadnezzar has ordered that you all be educated in the language and literature of Babylon. You've also earned the privilege to eat and drink from the king's table.

Daniel: We are Israelites. Our God has demanded that we not eat this food. Please, serve us something else.

Ashpenaz: I would love to do what you've asked me, but I fear my master, the king, who assigned your food; and when he sees that you have become paler and fainter than the other men, he will condemn me to death. Plus, everyone else loves eating what he serves.

(Ashpenaz leaves and Daniel and his friends talk.)

Shadrach: Daniel, what should we do? We can't eat the food or drink of the king!

Meshach: No! If we do, we would be disobeying God.

Abednego: But what will happen if we don't accept the food that has been offered?

Daniel: I don't know, but it doesn't matter what happens, I'll never eat or drink from the king's table!

Shadrach, Meshach and Abednego: Then neither will we!

Guard: It's almost time for dinner. Aren't you all excited! They are serving you food and drink from the king's table!

Daniel: Please, sir, can't you serve us

vegetables and water?

Guard: But, why do you want to eat only vegetables and drink only water when you can eat all of that?

Daniel: Because, this food will defile us.

Guard: Look, I just follow orders. Look at the others! They're enjoying the food. Just give it a try!

Daniel: Please test us for 10 days. Give us nothing but vegetables to eat and water to drink. Then compare us to the other young men who eat the royal food.

Guard: (whispering) We'll try this, but only for 10 days. After that you'll have to eat the royal food. I'm going to go find you some vegetables and water.

Narrator 1: After 10 days, Daniel and his friends had only eaten vegetables and had water to drink.

Shadrach: How do you feel Meshach?

Meshach: Fantastic!

Abednego: I agree! I'm imagining the face the guard will make when he sees us.

(The guard enters.)

Guard: The 10 days of trial have finished. Let's see how you guys look. Move closer to the window.

Daniel: What do you think?

Guard: Incredible! I wouldn't believe it if I wasn't seeing it with my own eyes!

Abednego: What is that supposed to mean?

Guard: That you guys look healthier and stronger than all of the other young men who have eaten the king's food!

Daniel: So, can we continue to eat our vegetables, sir?

Guard: Well of course! I'll order some more for all of you now.

Narrator 2: God blessed Daniel and his friends because they had the courage to remain steadfast in what they knew was right. God gave them knowledge and intelligence in reading and science.

Narrator 1: Three years later, the time had come for Daniel and his friends to be examined by King Nebuchadnezzar.

King Nebuchadnezzar: Ashpenaz! Have the four young men that you told me about come to me!

Ashpenaz: Yes, your majesty. At once!

Narrator 2: Ashpenaz brought Daniel and his friends before the king. The king talked to them and couldn't find anyone else in the group of prisoners quite like Daniel, Shadrach, Meshach, and Abednego; so, they remained in the service of the king. In any matter of wisdom or intelligence that the king consulted them on, he found them ten times better than all the magicians and astrologers that served in his kingdom.

(This Bible Story is found in Daniel 1.)

Be Like Daniel

Dare To Be Different!

I _____ have decided to stay firm in what I believe is good, even when others don't agree with me.

_____ _____
Signature   Date

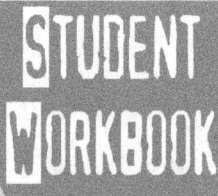

Lesson 8
STUDENT WORKBOOK

DECIDE TO MOVE FORWARD!

Memory Verse: "So whether you eat or drink or whatever you do, do it all for the glory of God." (1 Corinthians 10:31)

Giving In To Pressure

If your friends ask you to do something bad and you say NO, but they continue to pressure you, will you give in and do what they ask you?

Circle the number that you think best answers the questions.

If they laugh at you or call you names?

If they make you feel uncomfortable?

If they decide not to be your friend?

PROBABLY   MAYBE   NO
1 2 3 4 5

PROBABLY   MAYBE   NO
1 2 3 4 5

PROBABLY   MAYBE   NO
1 2 3 4 5

LET'S REBUILD THE WALL!

"Nehemiah, why are you so sad?" asked King Artaxerxes.

Nehemiah replied, *"Why should my face not look sad when the city where my ancestors are buried lies in ruins, and its gates have been destroyed by fire?"*

This city was Jerusalem. After king Nebuchadnezzar won the war against Judah, he burned God's temple and the doors into the city and tore down the walls.

The king asked Nehemiah, *"What is it you want?"*

Nehemiah prayed to God before he answered. He knew he had to be careful and say exactly what God wanted him to. *"If it pleases the king and if your servant has found favor in his sight, let him send me to the city in Judah where my ancestors are buried so that I can rebuild it."*

The king didn't want Nehemiah to leave because he was his cupbearer and he liked Nehemiah. But he gave permission for Nehemiah to go. When Nehemiah arrived in Jerusalem, no one was told what he had come to do. And one night when the moon was shining brilliantly, Nehemiah went out to inspect the wall and saw that is was in total ruins; there were no doors for its inhabitants to defend themselves against enemies.

The next day, Nehemiah got the whole city together and told them, *"You see the trouble we are in. Jerusalem is in ruins, and its gates have been burned with fire. Come, let us rebuild the walls of Jerusalem, and we'll no longer be in disgrace."*

The people replied, *"Let us start rebuilding."* And they began their work. Soon, some leaders of neighboring kingdoms heard what was happening. They didn't want Jerusalem to regain their strength and be a secured city again, so they went and tried to stop the construction.

They said, *"What is this you are doing? Are you rebelling against the king?"*

Nehemiah answered, *"The God of heaven will give us success."*

When Sanballat heard that they were re-building, he got angry. He made fun of Nehemiah and the people working with him. He asked, *"What are these feeble Jews doing?"*

Tobiah was at his side and said, *"What they are building – if even a fox climbed up on it, it would break down their wall of stones."*

Nehemiah and the city prayed and asked God to help them. So, they *rebuilt the wall until all of it reached half its height, for the people worked with all their heart.*

But when Sanballat, Tobiah, the Arabs, the Ammonites and the people of Ashdod heard that the repairs to Jerusalem's walls had gone ahead and that the gaps were being closed, they were very angry. They all plotted together to come and fight against Jerusalem and stir up trouble against it.

But Nehemiah and the people *prayed to our God and posted a guard day and night to meet this threat.*

Nehemiah said, *"Don't be afraid of them. Remember the Lord who is great and awesome, and fight for your families, your sons and your daughters, your wives and your homes."*

Afterwards, a few people from the city stayed on guard while others built the rest of the wall. Those who carried material did their work with one hand and held a weapon in the other. They worked every day until the stars came out.

They finished the wall in 52 days. When word came to Sanballat, Tobiah, Geshem the Arab and the rest of their enemies that Nehemiah had rebuilt the wall and not a gap was left in it, the other nations were humiliated and recognized that God had helped them in their work.

(This Bible Story is in Nehemiah 2, 4 & 6.)

Let's Build a Wall of PROTECTION

Do you want to become strong and be firm in doing only what is good and what God likes, even during times when someone mocks you or does not love you because you are a Christian?

If so, build your wall now!

Look up the following verses and match them with the corresponding phrase.

1 Read and Study your Bible.

2 Develop friendships and fellowship with other Christians.

3 Pray Every Day.

A. 1 Thessalonians 5:17

B. 1 Corinthians 15:33

C. James 1:22

Lesson 9

THE FAMILY OF THE COVENANT

Memory Verse: *"'Though the mountains be shaken and the hills be removed, yet my unfailing love for you won't be shaken nor my covenant of peace be removed,' says the Lord, who has compassion on you."* (Isaiah 54:10)

What Would You Do If God Told You...?

How would you feel? _____

What questions would you ask God? _____
_____
_____

What would you take with you? (List or draw the objects that you would take with you on the suitcase below.)

What would you have to leave behind? (List or draw the things you would have to leave behind on the trash can below.)

What would you miss the most? _____
_____
_____

"Go from your country, your people and your father's household to the land I'll show you." Genesis 12:1

37

An Agreement to Obey

Abram: Sarai, Lot, it's time for us to leave.

Servant 1: Where are we going? Why are we leaving? We like it here.

Abram: (in a strong voice directed toward his servants): Gather all of the sheep and cattle together. Guard everything we own. Lot and his family will also come with us. We are going to a new land that God will show us.

Servant 2: Let's hope God shows you a good land, my lord.

Narrator: Abram, Sarai his wife, and Lot took their families with them and went to the new land. (Walk together towards the other side of the room, which would be Canaan.)

Narrator: (Abram is walking): One day, the Lord appeared to Abram and said,

Voice of God: I'll give this land to your descendants.

Abram: (with a happy face): I'll build an altar to you, Jehovah! Because you have not only

given me this wonderful land, but you will give me a son.

Narrator: Many years passed. Abram waited patiently for God to fulfill His promise to give him a son; but he and his wife were getting older and they had no children.

Sarai: Abram, we are getting older every day. I don't think it is possible for us to have children anymore.

Abram: (embraces Sarai) Don't worry, Sarai, we must trust in God!

Narrator: Abram walks away from Sarai and God speaks to Abram.

Voice of God: Don't be afraid, Abram, I am your Creator and your reward will be great!

Abram: Lord, how will you keep your promises if you have not given me any children? You said that this land would belong to my children, but I don't have any children.

Narrator: God answered Abram,

Voice of God: Look up at the heavens and count the stars, can you count them all? That's how numerous your descendents will be.

Narrator: Abram and Sarai waited for a long time and still didn't have children. One day, Abram walked alone and God told him:

Voice of God: I'll make a covenant with you and multiply you greatly. You will no longer call yourself Abram. Your name will be Abraham, because I have made you the father of many nations. And your wife Sarai will now be called Sarah. Many nations and races will come from you. I'll establish a covenant with you forever and I'll be your God.

Abraham: (bowing down with his face to the ground) Lord, I am one hundred years old. How can I have a child at this age? My wife is ninety years old, how can she have a child?

What is a Covenant?

Unscramble the words to discover the definition of the word "Covenant".

A covenant is an **(ergmeenta)** _____.

God **(seforf)** _____ the covenant to His people. God's covenant makes it possible to have a **(oogd)** _____ **(slaterpihino)** _____ with Him.

The covenant of God **(fcetfas)** _____ **(ymna)** _____ people. God's covenant shows us His **(vole)** _____ and **(senufthifals)** _____.

The Formation of a Great Nation

Put a "T" for True or an "F" for false for each of the following statements.

1. _____ God initiated the covenant with Abraham.

2. _____ God chose Abraham to make the covenant with because Abraham was a good man.

3. _____ God told Abraham, "Don't leave your home so I can bless you."

4. _____ God didn't promise anything to Abraham in the covenant that they made.

5. _____ Abraham stayed calm the whole time that he waited for the son God had promised him.

God Keeps His Promises

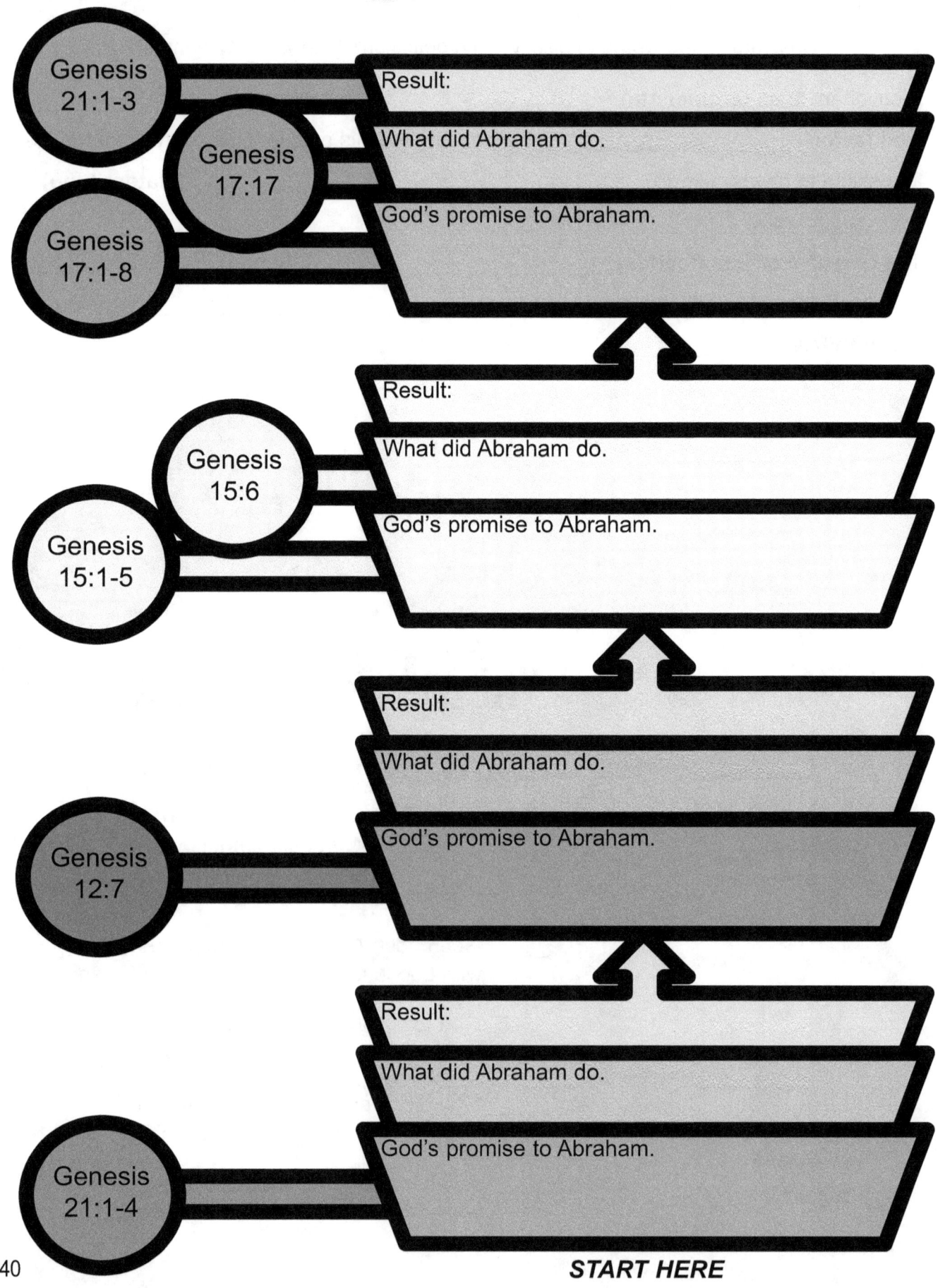

START HERE

40

Lesson 10 — Student Workbook

GOD'S COVENANT WITH HIS PEOPLE

Memory Verse: "'Though the mountains be shaken and the hills be removed, yet my unfailing love for you won't be shaken nor my covenant of peace be removed,' says the Lord, who has compassion on you." (Isaiah 54:10)

Responsibility?

What is a responsibility? _____
_____
_____
_____
_____

What responsibilities do you have? _____
_____
_____
_____
_____
_____

What responsibilities do children your age have? _____
_____
_____
_____

WE'LL DO WHAT THE LORD HAS SAID

Moses and all the Israelites set up their tents at the base of Mount Sinai. And Moses went up the mountain to meet God. Jehovah called to Moses from the mountain and said,

"This is what you are to say to the descendants of Jacob and what you are to tell the people of Israel, 'You yourselves have seen what I did to Egypt, and how I carried you on eagles' wings and brought you to myself. Now if you obey me fully and keep my covenant, then out of all nations you will be my treasured possession. Although the whole earth is mine, you will be for me a kingdom of priests and a holy nation.' These are the words you are to speak to the Israelites."

Then Moses went back to the people and summoned the elders and he told them what God had said. And they, in turn, spoke to the people and they told them what God had said. The people all responded together,

"We'll do everything the Lord has said."

"*On the morning of the third day, there was thunder and lightning, with a thick cloud over the mountain, and a very loud trumpet blast. Everyone in the camp trembled. Then Moses led the people out of the camp to meet with God, and they stood at the foot of the mountain.*"

"*And God spoke all these words,*

'I am the Lord your God, who brought you out of Egypt, out of the land of slavery. You shall have no other gods before me.'"

Moses told the people all that God had told him while he was on the mountain. God gave them the Ten Commandments and warned them what they should and shouldn't do in order to be a holy people.

(Italicized words are quotes from Exodus 19:3-6,8,16-17; 20:1-3)

A Formal Covenant

Read Exodus 19:4-8 and complete the following paragraph by filling in each blank with the missing word:

" 'You yourselves have _____ what I did to Egypt, and how I _____ you on _____ wings and brought you to _____. Now if you _____ fully and keep my _____, then out of all the nations you will be my _____ _____. Although the whole earth is _____, you will be for me a _____ of _____ and a _____ nation.' The people responded together, 'We _____ do everything the _____ has said.' "

RESPONSBILITIES OF THE PEOPLE OF GOD

Make a list of responsibilities that are based on these commandments.

COMMANDMENT   RESPONSIBILITY

2nd Commandment _____

4th Commandment _____

5th Commandment _____

8th Commandment _____

9th Commandment _____

Lesson 11

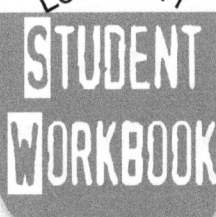

A NEW COVENANT

Memory Verse: " *'Though the mountains be shaken and the hills be removed, yet my unfailing love for you won't be shaken nor my covenant of peace be removed,' says the Lord, who has compassion on you.*" (Isaiah 54:10)

Complete the following verse by filling in the blanks using the Bible references below.

When the _____ came, Jesus and his _____ reclined at the _____. And he said to them, 'I have eagerly desired to _____ this _____ with you before I suffer.' . . . And he took _____, gave thanks and broke it, and gave it to them, saying, 'This is my _____ given for you; do this in remembrance of me.' In the same way, after the supper he took the _____, saying, 'This is the new _____ in my _____, which is _____ _____ for you.' "

Luke 22:14-15,19-20

45

A New Covenant

When the people of Israel were enslaved in Egypt, God promised to deliver them, and in order to do that he sent the ten plagues. The last of the plagues was the death of the firstborn son.

In order for the firstborn of the Israelites to survive, they were instructed to kill lambs without blemish, the best of the flock, and with the blood of this animal paint the threshold (the edges) of the doors to their houses. They were to prepare a meal using bitter herbs and unleavened bread. This became a yearly celebration called Passover, which was to remind the Israelites of how God freed them from Egypt.

When Jesus came to earth he also celebrated the Passover with his disciples, but in a different way. He told his disciples, *"I have eagerly desired to eat this Passover with you before I suffer. Take this and divide it among you. This is my body given for you; do this in remembrance of me. This cup is the new covenant of my blood, which is poured out for you."*

THE LAST SUPPER

What is the New Covenant?

1. What is a Covenant? _____
   _____
   _____

2. What was the "Old Covenant"? _____
   _____
   _____

3. Look up Hebrews 8:13 and fill in the missing words in the following verse.

   "By calling this covenant "_____," he [Christ] has made the _____ one _____; and what is obsolete and _____ will soon _____."

New People in the Old Covenant made by God

Cutout the branch, write your name on the line and paste it on the tree.

The old covenant was made with the people of Israel, and although we are not Israelites, we have been made part of God's covenant. In Romans 11:11-24, it says that those who were not part of the people of Israel have been grafted into the tree of the chosen family. If you have accepted Christ as your Savior, you are part of the special people of God.

Lesson 12

JESUS, A DIFFERENT KING

Memory Verse: "...that at the name of Jesus every knee should bow, in heaven and on earth and under the earth..." (Philippians 2:10)

Who is the king that is coming?

Take an imaginary trip back in time:

Mario is a boy your age and he is visiting Jerusalem almost 2,000 years ago. He sees a big crowd of people and follows it to see what all the commotion is about.

Suddenly he finds himself next to a Pharisee and he asks,

Mario: Sir, Where are all these people going?

Pharisee: It seems that an extraordinary man is arriving and they have come to see him.

Mario: Why do they want to see him?

Pharisee: Because they believe he is the Messiah, the one that the prophets said would be the king of Israel.

Mario: Wow! Do you believe that he is the King?

Pharisee: Of course not! How could that be? Jesus is only the son of a poor carpenter from Nazareth, and as you know, nothing good comes from there.

Mario: Why do the people want a king? We already have one.

Pharisee: Because they want someone who will free them from Roman rule.

Mario: And you believe that Jesus can do that?

Pharisee: How could Jesus free them? He doesn't have an army, just a few disciples. I don't appreciate the Romans either but it could be worse. At least they keep the peace and let us worship as we please. I only hope that Jesus doesn't cause any problems.

Mario: Look! He is riding on a donkey. Isn't that what kings do when they coming into a city in peace?

Pharisee: No, a king wouldn't arrive riding on a donkey.

Mario: Listen! Why are the

people shouting "Hosanna"? Does "Hosanna" mean "Save Us"?

Pharisee: Yes, this is blasphemy! But soon they will realize that Jesus is not a king. He won't save them from the Romans. He will be lucky if he can save himself.

"Is he coming?" asked a man.

"Yes!" said another. "He's not far from the city."

There were a lot of people in Jerusalem. Large crowds who had come to Jerusalem to celebrate the Passover Feast. Upon hearing that Jesus was coming to Jerusalem, they took palm branches and went out to meet him.

"Look! Jesus is riding on a donkey. It's exactly how the prophet Zechariah said that it would happen, 'Fear not, daughter of Zion; Your King comes, seated on a donkey's colt.' Jesus is the Messiah! Hosanna!"

"Blessed is he who comes in the name of the Lord, the King of Israel!" cried the crowd.

People cut palm branches and waved them. Some put them on the ground and made a path for Jesus.

"Is this the man who raised Lazarus?" a woman asked her friend.

"Yes!" her friend answered. "I was visiting Martha, Lazarus' sister, and I saw it! Jesus commanded Lazarus to come out of the tomb, and he had been dead for days."

THE KING IS COMING

"Anyone who resurrects someone is greater than the Romans and their armies," said another woman. "Surely Jesus will become king. He will defeat the Romans."

"I heard that his father, Joseph, is from the house of David. Perhaps this is how God will fulfill his promise to David. If Jesus becomes King, one of the descendants of David will have the throne! Is this not exactly what God promised David so many years ago?"

"Jesus must be the king that God promised us."

The crowd shouted again and again, "Hosanna! Hosanna!"

The Pharisees and other religious leaders were angry.

"This is all out of control. If Herod or the Romans find out, they will punish us all." So the Pharisees plotted to kill Jesus.

The King of kings

When Jesus made his triumphal entry into Jerusalem, the Jews thought that he would be their king. But the cross showed them that they had the wrong idea about Jesus and his ministry. On a piece of paper, draw a symbol that represents what Jesus really suffered. If you need clues, you can read John 19:2.

What Should A King Do?

Palm branch leaves:
- Punish the bad guys
- Heal all the sick
- Restore the glory of King David
- Lead the armies of Israel
- Ensure that justice is carried out.
- Become the High Priest in order to bring his people back to God.
- Take care of the poor
- Deliver the Jews from the Roman Empire
- Be forever King of the people of God
- Save God's people from their sins.

When Jesus entered Jerusalem, the crowd cheered for him, thinking that he would be their king. They welcomed him with palm branches. But they had misconceptions about what Jesus came to do. In the leaves of this palm branch appear things that the people thought the Messiah would do. Draw a ♥ (heart) next to the things that Jesus did, and an X next to the things that Jesus didn't come to do.

52

JESUS, THE RISEN KING

Memory Verse: *"At the name of Jesus every knee should bow, in heaven and on earth and under the earth."* (Philippians 2:10)

The last days in Jerusalem were very sad. Jesus was taken as a prisoner and subjected to several interrogations. He was unfairly tried and taken to be crucified on Friday.

Jewish law said that the body should be buried before the Sabbath, because that was a special day for the Jews, the day of rest.

That's why, when they arrived on Sunday, they wanted to go to the tomb.

Try to imagine that you have to go to the tomb to finish preparing Jesus' body for burial. How would you have felt while you were walking to the tomb?

Draw on the face what your expression would have been and write in the thought bubble what you might have thought as you walked to Jesus' tomb.

WALKING TO THE TOMB

He Lives!

Jesus' disciples and their friends were very sad because they had seen him die on the cross. Let's see how they felt on Sunday morning when they made a discovery that changed history.

"They have stolen the body of Jesus, it's no longer in the tomb!" cried Mary Magdalene, hurrying out. She went to meet Simon Peter and the other disciple and said to them, "They have taken the Lord out of the tomb, and we don't know where they have put him!"

"Calm down, Mary. Tell us what has happened?" Peter said.

"I went to the tomb early this morning and when I arrived I saw that the huge stone which sealed the tomb had been moved and the tomb was open. I looked inside and the Master's body was not there; someone must have taken it.

Peter and the other disciple left and went to the tomb. They ran together, but the other disciple ran faster than Peter and reached the tomb first. Then, Simon Peter came behind him, entered the tomb, and saw strips of linen lying there along with the shroud which had covered Jesus' head.

The two men were stunned; what had happened to the body of Christ? They had to decide what they were going to do. The disciples returned to their homes.

Now Mary stood outside the tomb crying. As she wept, she bent over to look into the tomb and saw two angels in white, seated where Jesus' body had been, one at the head and the other at the foot. They asked her,

"Woman, why are you crying?"

She replied, "They have taken my Lord away, and I don't know where they have put him."

Having said this, she turned and saw Jesus standing there; but she didn't know it was Jesus.

Then Jesus said to her, "Woman, why are you crying? Who is it you are looking for?"

Mary didn't yet recognize Jesus, she thought he was the gardener, and she said to him, "Sir, if you have carried him away, tell me where you have put him, and I'll get him."

"Jesus said to her, 'Mary!'"

"Is it true?" Mary wondered when she heard her name. "Yes it's him! He is alive!" "Teacher!" Mary cried.

Jesus said, "Go to my disciples and tell them that I live. Tell them, 'I am ascending to my Father and your Father, to my God and your God.'"

Again Mary ran to go and get the disciples.

"Jesus lives!" she said to herself. "They'll all be happy when they hear the news. Jesus really lives!"

Then Mary Magdalene went to give the disciples the news that she had seen the Lord.

(This story is found in John 20.)

A REASON... TO REJOICE

Now imagine that when you arrive at the tomb you hear the good news that Jesus has risen. Draw on the face what your reaction to that good news would be. Then write in the thought bubble what you would have thought.

OUR RISEN KING

With the help of your teacher, make a list of how the disciples felt and what they believed about Jesus, before the resurrection and after the resurrection.

Before the Resurrection:	After the Resurrection:

Jesus was resurrected for you and for me. He is our resurrected King. Read John 14:19 and find the promise Jesus makes to those who believe in him.

"Because I live, _____." John 14:19b

56 *With Love, Jesus*

Lesson 14

STUDENT WORKBOOK

JESUS, A FORGIVING KING

Memory Verse: *"At the name of Jesus, every knee should bow, in heaven and on earth and under the earth."* (Philippians 2:10)

How Could You?

"I thought you were my friend?"

What do you think happened to make this girl feel rejected by her friend? How do you feel when a friend does something or says something that offends you?

The Return

Narrator: Peter took a stone, threw it hard and saw it fall into the sea.

Peter: Ah, the sea of Tiberias! What beautiful memories I have of the times I came to fish on these beaches! So many things have happened lately! The arrest of Jesus, his crucifixion . . . finally, terrible things.

I'll never forget what happened. Jesus appeared to us a third time in this same place. He even served us breakfast.

Then he said to me, "Simon, son of John, do you love me more than these?" I was surprised by the question, but I said, "Yes Lord, you know that I love you!"

Jesus said to me, "Feed my lambs."

I miss the company of Jesus a lot. But you know what? Again he asked me, "Do you love me?" I couldn't understand why he asked me again, but I replied firmly, "Yes Lord, you know that I love you!" Jesus said to me, "Take care of my sheep."

Underline the correct answer to each question:

1. When did Jesus and Peter have this conversation?
   a. Before the crucifixion
   b. After the resurrection

2. What did Jesus mean when he asked Peter, "Do you love me more than these?"
   a. That Peter loved Jesus more than he loved anyone else.
   b. That Peter was the best disciple.

# of Peter

However, after the second question, I began to remember things that had happened recently, when suddenly Jesus fixed his eyes on me and asked me again, "Simon, son of John, do you love me?"

I couldn't answer, I remembered that I had not been a loyal friend to him, I had denied him! I didn't deny him once, but three times. In the most difficult moments I was not with him.

I got up quickly and stretched out my arms for his forgiveness and said, "Lord, you know everything, you know that I love you." But this time, I said it with great humility, recognizing that Jesus' love for me was much greater than what I felt for him. Jesus said to me, "Feed my sheep."

Narrator: Peter always remembered this scene, but not with sadness, but with deep gratitude to the Lord for his mercy. He became one of the disciples who worked hard to spread the gospel.

3. What was Jesus asking Peter to do when he said, "Feed my sheep"?
   a. To guide his followers.
   b. To represent Christ on earth.

4. How many times did Jesus ask Peter this question?
   a. Six
   b. Three

Lesson 15 — STUDENT WORKBOOK

JESUS, THE LIVING KING

Memory Verse: *"At the name of Jesus every knee should bow, in heaven and on earth and under the earth."* (Philippians 2:10)

It's a Spirit!

Narrator: It's the third day since the crucifixion of Jesus. Ten of his disciples are talking in a room. The doors are closed and locked because they are afraid of the authorities.

James: All of this is so confusing. We saw Jesus die. We saw him buried.

Andrew: Yes, and a large stone covered the entrance of the tomb. They sealed it and put soldiers there to guard it.

James: But Mary Magdalene says she saw Jesus, and that he spoke to her early this morning.

Andrew: Peter and John went to the tomb. They saw that the stone to the entrance of the tomb was rolled to one side and that the tomb was empty.

Peter: Yes! The tomb was empty and the grave clothes were left there!

John (thoughtfully): The shroud covering the face of Jesus was perfectly folded and separated from the rest of the cloth.

Peter: Exactly!

Andrew: And now Cleopas and his friend, who were going to Emmaus, say that they saw Jesus on the road.

James: And not only that! They invited him to dinner with them! And when He blessed the bread, they recognized Him.

Andrew: What does all of this mean?

Narrator: At that very moment, Jesus appears among them and spoke to them.

Jesus: Peace to you!

James: It's a spirit!

Andrew: Yes, it's a ghost!

Jesus: Why are you troubled and why do doubts rise to your mind? Look at my hands and my feet, I am myself. Touch me and see, a spirit or ghost does not have flesh and bones, as you see I have.

Andrew: Look! There are the scars of the nails with which they crucified Him!

Peter: It looks so real! Maybe we're all dreaming.

James: It's too good to be true!

Jesus: Do you have something to eat?

John: Yes, here is some fish left over from dinner.

Peter: Look, he's eating! A spirit cannot eat!

James: Jesus is alive!

John: Yes, he has risen!

Jesus: This is what I told you while I was still with you: Everything must be fulfilled that is written about me in the Law of Moses, the Prophets and the Psalms.

Andrew: It's Jesus, there's no doubt about it!

Narrator: Then Jesus opened their minds so they could understand the Scriptures.

Jesus: This is what is written: The Messiah will suffer and rise from the dead on the third day, and repentance for the forgiveness of sins will be preached in his name to all nations, beginning at Jerusalem.

All Together: We'll do everything you say, Lord!

THEY SAW HIM!

A Roman solder, sent to guard the tomb of Jesus. ;
(Matthew 27:65; 28:4)

Mary Magdalene
(John 20:11-16)

The disciples had trouble believing that Jesus was alive until they saw him with their own eyes. After they saw him, they all wanted to talk about the good news.

Choose one of the characters below. Read the Bible verse for the one you chose and write in the bubble what that person told others about Jesus.

Cleopas traveling to Emmaus

(Luke 24:13 -16, 28 -31)

Simon Peter.

(John: 20:1-7)

JESUS LIVES TODAY!

After Jesus was resurrected, he never died again. He lives today!! Read the Bible verses below and discover what He is doing now. Write on the postcard what Jesus is doing for people today.

Matthew 28:19-20
John 14:1-4
1 John 2:1

Lesson 16

STUDENT WORKBOOK

JESUS, THE KING OF KINGS

Memory Verse: *"At the name of Jesus every knee should bow, in heaven and on earth and under the earth."* (Philippians 2:10)

The Kings That People Follow

A king is someone or something that people put first in their lives. Look at the children on the left. Do you see the flags in their hands? Who is king for each child?

Write under each flag who the king is for each child.

Now draw on the blank flag a person or object that is very important to children your age, someone whom they try to follow as if they were king.

Jesus, Our King Who Ascended!

It was late, Peter and Andrew could not sleep.

"These last forty days have been incredible," Peter said. "So many things have happened! I can't help but wonder what could be waiting for us next."

"I know what you mean, Peter," Andrew said.

"When we believed that Jesus would be crowned king, great problems began. I'll never forget the fear I felt when the soldiers took Jesus away. Nor can I stop thinking about how he suffered."

"We were very afraid of the Romans, too!" said Peter.

"Yes, and now we're more afraid of them. The news of Jesus' resurrection is spreading throughout Jerusalem. The city officials find themselves increasingly angry, trying to hide the truth of the resurrection; they say that one of us stole his body. But let them say what they want. Jesus is alive! We have seen Him and so have many people in different places. How can they deny that he is the Messiah?"

"I'm still very afraid of what the Romans will do to us if we don't keep quiet," Andrew said.

Peter asked, "Do you remember the words of Jesus before he was crucified? He said, *"Don't let your hearts be troubled. You believe in God; believe also in me."*

Andrew relaxed, sighed and said, "I remember something else that Jesus told us; He said that he was going to his Father's house. Peter, do you remember his words? *"I am going there to prepare a place for you . . . I'll come back and take you to be with me that you also may be where I am."*

"I've thought about that a lot," Peter said. "And I also remember what he told us when he ate with us, "Don't leave Jerusalem, but wait for the gift my Father promised ... but in a few days you will be baptized with the Holy Spirit.""

Andrew looked confused. "Yes, I know," he said. "I'm not sure what he meant, but did you hear how he talked about his kingdom?"

Then those who were gathered around him asked, "Lord, are you at this time going to restore the kingdom to Israel?" "It is not for you to know the times or dates the Father has set by his own authority. But you will receive power when the Holy Spirit comes on you; and you will be my witnesses in Jerusalem, and in all Judea and Samaria, and to the ends of the earth."

"After he said this, he was taken up before their very eyes, and a cloud hid him from their sight. They were looking intently up into the sky as he was going, when suddenly two men dressed in white stood beside them. "Men of Galilee," they said, "why do you stand here looking into the sky? This same Jesus, who has been taken from you into heaven, will come back in the same way you have seen him go into heaven.""

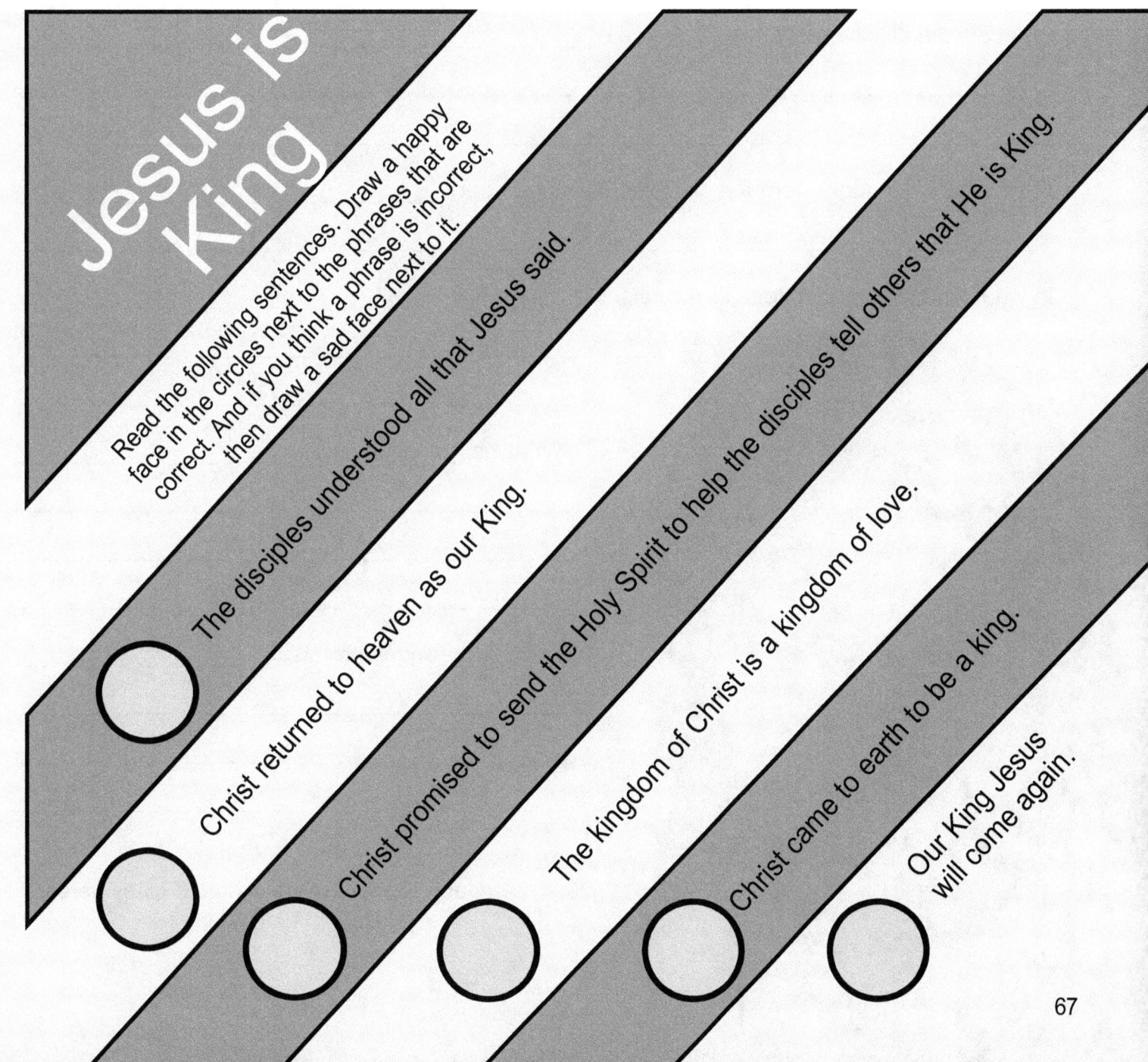

Jesus is King

Read the following sentences. Draw a happy face in the circles next to the phrases that are correct. And if you think a phrase is incorrect, then draw a sad face next to it.

- The disciples understood all that Jesus said.
- Christ returned to heaven as our King.
- Christ promised to send the Holy Spirit to help the disciples tell others that He is King.
- The kingdom of Christ is a kingdom of love.
- Christ came to earth to be a king.
- Our King Jesus will come again.

Let's Review
(Your teacher will tell you what you need to do for this activity.)

- How many days was Jesus with his disciples after his resurrection? _____
_____

- How do you think the disciples felt to have Jesus with them? _____
_____

- Did Jesus demonstrated great power when he rose from the dead? _____

- What did Jesus promise? _____
_____

- What did the disciples ask Jesus? (verse 6) _____
_____
_____

- What kind of kingdom were the disciples thinking about? _____
_____

- In what kind of kingdom does Jesus reign? _____
_____
_____

- What happened next? _____
_____
_____
_____

- What did the angels promise? _____
_____
_____
_____

Now, compare your answers with your classmates.

Lesson 17

STUDENT WORKBOOK

JESUS, THE RETURNING KING

Memory Verse: *"At the name of Jesus every knee should bow, in heaven and on earth and under the earth."* (Philippians 2:10)

A Close Inspection

Would you like to live here forever? Why and Why not?

Hope and Wellbeing

The disciples loved Jesus as an intimate friend. They recognized him as the Messiah, and were filled with fear and confusion when he was arrested. Afterwards, he was subjected to interrogation, to different punishments, and finally crucified. On Friday afternoon, Jesus died on the cross and was buried. The disciples were very sad and scared because they didn't know what would happen next. On the third day after he died, they discovered that his tomb was empty. That filled them with excitement and joy. Then Jesus appeared to them several times, talking to them about many topics to help them understand who He was and what would happen in the future.

Read Acts 1:4-8. What promise did Jesus make to his disciples? How would God help them after Jesus had gone to heaven?
Now read Acts 1:9-11. What promise did the angels make to the disciples when Jesus ascended to heaven?

How do you think the disciples felt about what the angels said? We were not there when Jesus ascended to heaven, so we just can't imagine how they must have felt. It is possible that we may be alive when Christ returns. Read Matthew 25:31-45 and 1 Thessalonians 4:13-18.

| A period of three years | A Sad Night | A Dark Day | The Resurrection  |

How do you feel when you think that

God's Timing

Jesus' Return

The Arrest of Jesus

Jesus' Ministry

The coming of the Holy Spirit

Jesus' Ascension

The Crucifixion

Cut out the boxes, on the right, that represent events that are important to Christians. Then glue them in the correct order that they happened, in the timeline below. Draw yourself in the space the represents where we are in the timeline.

About 40 days after the crucifixion	The Promised Gift		A Future Event

you may be alive when Christ returns?

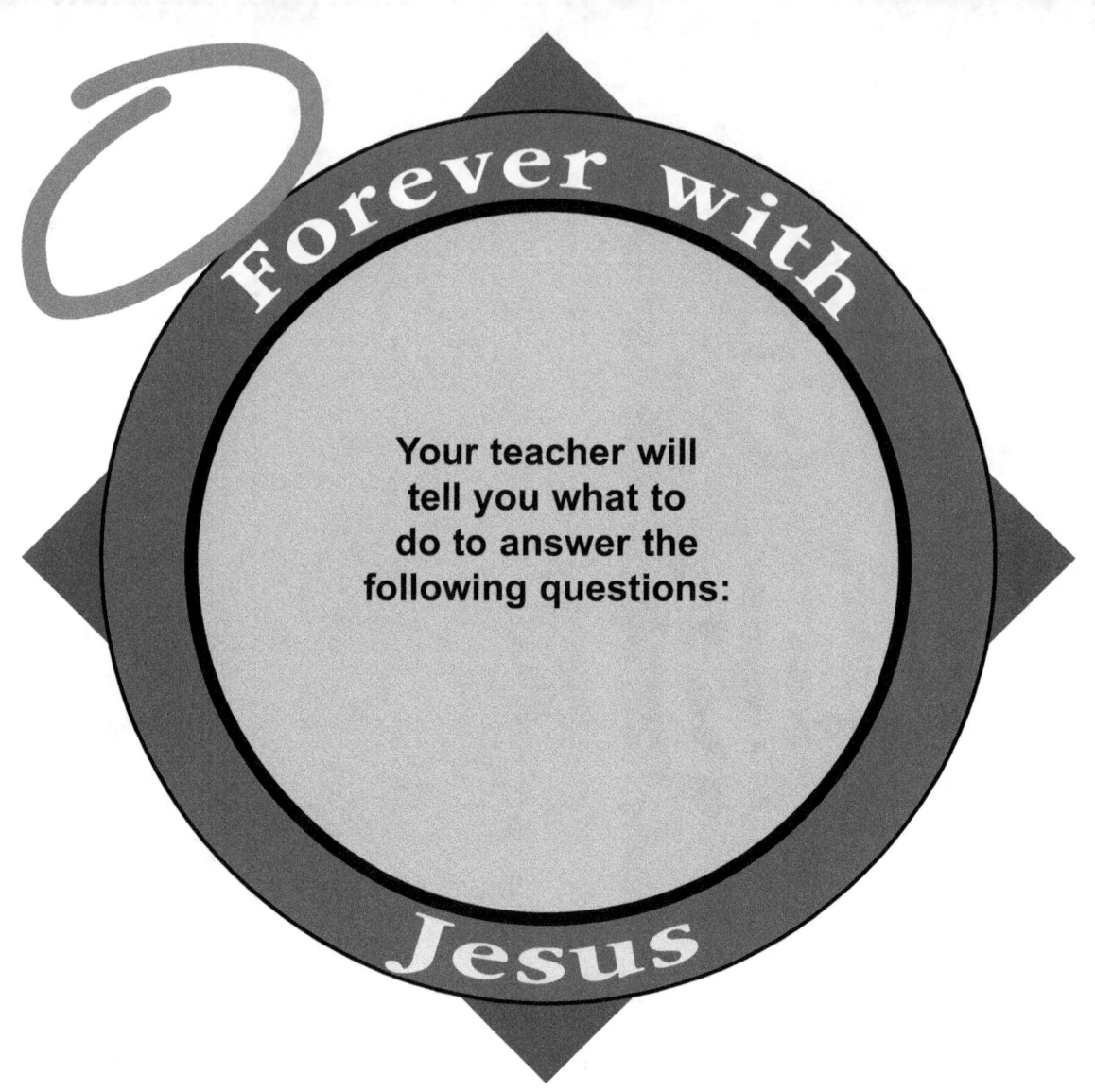

Forever with Jesus

Your teacher will tell you what to do to answer the following questions:

How many days was Jesus with his disciples after his resurrection? _____

What did Jesus do during those forty days? _____

What did Jesus tell them before he left? _____

What was that promise? _____

What would the Holy Spirit give? _____

Where would they be witnesses? _____

When Jesus ascended to heaven, what did the angels say? _____

How do you think the disciples felt? _____

Lesson 18

STUDENT WORKBOOK

THE BIRTH OF THE CHURCH

Memory Verse: *"Now you are the body of Christ, and each one of you is a part of it."* (1 Corinthians 12:27)

A Silhouette of a Human Body

LIKE A STRONG WIND

Jesus' disciples were sitting together, talking about what they would do now that Jesus had ascended to heaven.

"I want to get out of Jerusalem," one of them said. "I'm tired of waiting for something to happen. If the Romans decide to come after us, they will easily find us!"

"We can't go," said another. "Jesus said to us, 'Don't leave Jerusalem, but wait for the promise of the Father.'"

"But how long do we have to wait?"

"I thought Jesus would be back soon! And it's been a week since we saw him go to heaven; And these men dressed in white told us that he would come again, in the same way that he left. I think we should go to the place where we saw him ascend. What do you think?"

"Jesus told us to wait in Jerusalem, and that's where I'm going to stay!" said Peter, standing among the crowd of 120, encouraging them to continue praying. He said to them, "Jesus promised us that after the Holy Spirit comes, we'll be witnesses for him. Please have patience."

As the group prayed, suddenly a sound came from the sky, like a strong wind blowing, and it filled the whole house.

"What is that?" they wanted to know.

Then tongues like fire appeared, resting on each one of them. And they were all filled with the Holy Spirit. Outside were Jews from all the nations under heaven visiting Jerusalem. When they heard the noise, many went to where the disciples were to see what was happening.

They were astonished and amazed, saying, *"Aren't all these who are speaking Galileans? Then how is it that each of us hears them in our native language?"*

"This is incredible!" said another.

Others mocked the disciples and said, "They must be drunk."

Then Peter proudly stood up, and with a loud voice began to preach to them.

"Fellow Jews and all of you who live in Jerusalem, let me explain this to you; listen carefully to what I say. These people are not drunk. If you had listened to what the prophets said, you would know that God promised to send His Spirit to all people, and this is what is happening here today."

"Therefore, let all Israel be assured of this: God has made this Jesus, whom you crucified, both Lord and Messiah."

"Oh no!" cried some. "We crucified the Promised One!" Then they asked the apostles, *"Brothers, what shall we do?"*

Peter said to them, *"Repent and be baptized, every one of you, in the name of Jesus Christ for the forgiveness of your sins. And you will receive the gift of the Holy Spirit."*

"Those who accepted his message were baptized, and about three thousand were added to their number that day."

(Italicized words are quotes from the NIV Bible.)

A Big Change!

Before

After

Something happened to Peter. Look at the two cartoons and write what Peter said in the speech bubbles. How could it be so different? What caused the big change?

He Makes the Difference

Who is the Holy Spirit?

The church uses many names and symbols to refer to the Holy Spirit.

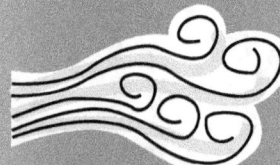

"COMFORTER"

Write next to each symbol what it represents about the Holy Spirit.

The Birth of the Church

WORDSEARCH

Search for the hidden words. They may go in any direction.

```
B A C J N D F I R E Y T W I N D J R
J U D E A Q P P R A Y E R H G I P S
P C D R T F O R G I V E N E S S E L
R H Y U I L S P I R I T D B N C K E
O U R S O K B J E S U S C H R I S T
M R L A N G U A G E S A C E J P B Y
I C E L S C P O W E R A Y H O L Y M
S H R E P E R S E V E R A N C E O R
E S A M A R I A B W I T N E S S E S
```

CHURCH	NATIONS
DISCIPLES	PERSEVERANCE
FIRE	POWER
FORGIVENESS	PRAYER
HOLY	PROMISE
JERUSALEM	SAMARIA
JESUS CHRIST	SPIRIT
JUDEA	WIND
LANGUAGES	WITNESSES

76

Lesson 19

GOD'S LOVE WITHIN THE CHURCH

Memory Verse: *"Now you are the body of Christ, and each one of you is a part of it."* (1 Corinthians 12:27)

CHRISTIAN FRIENDSHIP CLUB

Who are the people you can always count on? Imagine that you are starting a special club called The Christian Friendship Club. What rules would you like this club to have? Create an advertisement for the club and include those rules.

Welcome to the: Christian Friendship Club

Club Rules:

Jesus' Best Friends

"Peter, can you come to my house today?" a new convert asked. "My friends and I would like to speak with you about Jesus. You know so much about him and his teachings."

After Peter's first sermon, 3,000 new Christians needed a place to grow stronger in their faith. They devoted themselves to the apostles' teachings, to fellowship with one another, and to the breaking of bread and to prayer. They were filled with awe at the many signs and wonders performed by the apostles.

People gathered in the temple to worship. Some small groups met in houses. Sometimes people meet in a place outside the temple called "The Porch of Solomon" to tell each other their problems, and to enjoy time together.

"Hello Joseph!" said Matthew, "is there anything I can do for you?"

"I'm fine, thank you," replied Joseph. "I just came to give you something. I sold some of my property and would like to give the money to someone who needs it."

"Thank you, Joseph," said the apostle, "We will call you Barnabas instead of Joseph, because Barnabas means 'Son of Encouragement', and it's a perfect name for a man as generous as you are."

Joseph smiled.

The multitude who believed what Peter shared were of one heart and one soul. None of them said that they had anything of their own, but they shared everything with each other.

Then Joseph said, "I am not the only one who has sold their property to help those in need. We all must love and help each other, just as Jesus commanded."

The Power of Friendship

1. Why was Juan sad? _____
_____

2. Why did Miguel want to help Juan? _____
_____

3. How did Miguel help Juan? _____
_____

4. What was the result of his action? _____
_____

5. How does this story relate to the life of the early Christians as recorded in Acts 2:43-47?
_____
_____

6. What made it possible for there to be fellowship among these people? _____
_____
_____

7. How can we become friends and have fellowship with others? ____
_____
_____

8. What do we need for there to be true Christian fellowship? _____
_____

9. What else do you need to have true Christian fellowship? _____
_____
_____

Discover the Bible Verse!

1 = a	6 = f	11 = k	16 = p	21 = u	26 = z
2 = b	7 = g	12 = l	17 = q	22 = v	
3 = c	8 = h	13 = m	18 = r	23 = w	
4 = d	9 = i	14 = n	19 = s	24 = x	
5 = e	10 = j	15 = o	20 = t	25 = y	

1 12 12   20 8 5   2 5 12 9 5 22 5 18 19   23 5 18 5
_____   _____   _____   _____

15 14 5   9 14   8 5 1 18 20   1 14 4   13 9 14 4.
_____ ____ _____ _____ _____.

14 15   15 14 5   3 12 1 9 13 5 4   20 8 1 20   1 14 25
_____ _____   _____   _____   _____

15 6   20 8 5 9 18   16 15 19 19 5 19 19 9 15 14 19
____   _____   _____

23 1 19   20 8 5 9 18   15 23 14,   2 21 20
_____   _____   _____,   _____

20 8 5 25   19 8 1 18 5 4   5 22 5 18 25 20 8 9 14 7
_____   _____   _____

20 8 5 25   8 1 4.   1 3 20 19   .
_____   ____.   _____   4:32

Lesson 20

STUDENT WORKBOOK

WE OBEY GOD

Memory Verse: *"Now you are the body of Christ, and each one of you is a part of it."* (1 Corinthians 12:27)

PRISON BARS

Why do people get locked up in a prison?
_____
_____
_____
_____

Do you think those people deserve to be there?
_____
_____
_____
_____

Why or why not?
_____
_____
_____
_____

Do you think that someone has ever been imprisoned for doing something good?
_____
_____
_____
_____

Who Went To Jail?

Narrator: Peter and John walked towards the temple.

Peter: Hey, John, what time is it?

John: Almost three. We must go to the temple to pray.

Narrator: Peter and John walked towards the temple. As they arrived, they saw a lame man sitting next to the gate that was called "Beautiful."

John: Why are you sitting here?

Lame man: I can't walk, I was born like this. I can't work to earn money, so I sit here and ask those who come to the temple to help me. Do you have money to give me?

John: I'm sorry, but I don't have any money. Do you, Peter?

Peter: Silver or gold I don't have, but what I do have I give you. In the name of Jesus Christ of Nazareth, walk.

Narrator (with enthusiasm): Then he took him by the right hand and lifted him up. Immediately his feet and ankles straightened. Jumping up, he stood and walked. He went with them into the temple, walking, leaping, and praising God. All the people were astonished at what had happened.

Peter: Israelites, why do you marvel at this? Why do you set your eyes on us, as if by our power we have made him walk?

Narrator: However, not everyone was happy that the lame man was healed. The rulers of the temple were very angry.

Temple leader: What are you doing here? Who gave you permission to teach? We don't like what you say about Jesus. We all know he was crucified. We don't want you to tell more stories about him being resurrected! Either you stop talking, or we'll put you in jail!

Narrator: Then the soldiers took Peter and John and threw them into prison. But many of those who had heard their message believed, and their number grew to about 5,000 men. The next day, they brought Peter and John to the Council. The man who was healed was standing there too. The priests began to question the apostles.

Temple leader: By what power or in what name have you done this?

Peter: In the name of Jesus Christ of Nazareth, whom you crucified and whom God raised from the dead, through him this man stands before you, healed.

Narrator: Then, seeing the courage of Peter and John, they recognized that they had been with Jesus.

Temple leader: Gentlemen, we give you your freedom on the condition that you refrain from preaching and teaching about Jesus. Do you understand this?

Peter and John: Which is right in God's eyes: to listen to you, or to him? You be the judges! As for us, we cannot help speaking about what we have seen and heard.

Narrator: After that, the rulers of the temple could not think of anything to say or do. They could not decide how to punish them, because all the people were praising God for what had happened. So, after threatening them, they let them go free. Peter and John went to their fellow believers and told them all that had happened to them.

Persecuted Christians Hall Of Fame

Throughout history, many Christians have been persecuted because of their faith in Jesus Christ. Search the Bible verses below and write down why these heroes were persecuted.

Jesus — John 19:1-6

Stephen — Acts 7:56-60

Paul — 2 Corinthians 11:23-27

Whose place is this? — 2 Timothy 3:12

Persecution
HOW TO SURVIVE

Over time, bad people have tried to destroy the church, and they have done horrible things to Christians, hoping that the rest of the Christians would be afraid to believe. But the church has survived and continues to grow. Equip yourself so that you won't to be suddenly surprised.

1. Don't be taken by surprise! Make a list of situations in which you could be persecuted for what you believe.

2. What was the secret of the courage of Jesus, Peter, John, Stephen and Paul?

3. How can the Christian community help make persecution more bearable?

4. What can you do to protect yourself? Read Ephesians 6:10-18.

5. Why must we face persecution with honor? Read Matthew 5:11-12.

Lesson 21

STUDENT WORKBOOK

NOTHING CAN STOP THE CHURCH!

Memory Verse: *"Now you are the body of Christ, and each one of you is a part of it."* (1 Corinthians 12:27)

FIND THE WAY OUT

Help the Apostles find their way to freedom now that the angel has freed them from prison.

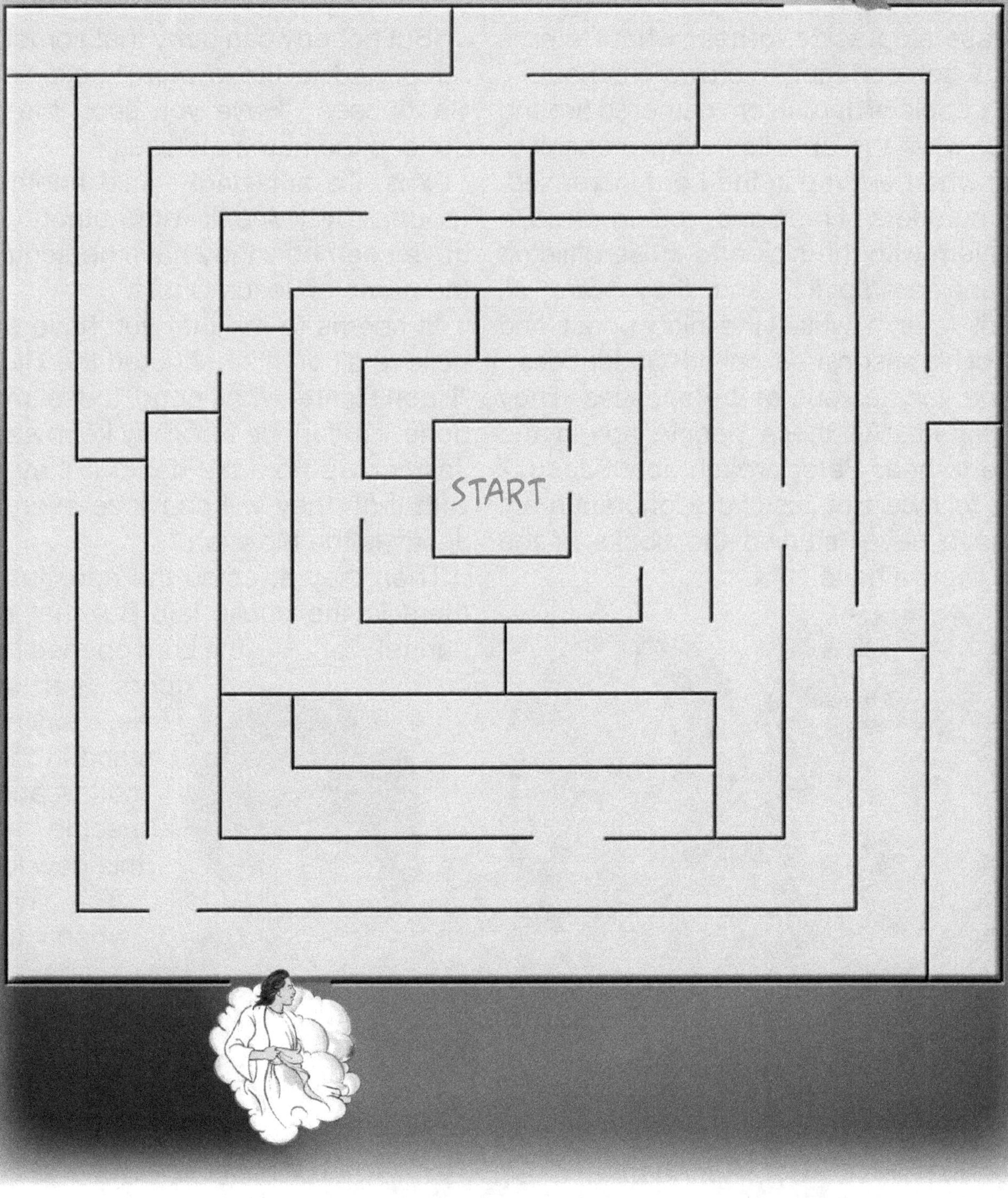

START

85

You Can't Stop Them!

"Please step aside to hear what Peter is saying!" someone in the crowd cried out.

The people of Jerusalem gathered around to hear what the apostles were preaching. Those who believed in the Lord increased. Large numbers of men and women came to Jerusalem with the sick and those afflicted with unclean spirits, and they were all healed. After a while, the high priest and some of his associates, called "Sadducees," became very jealous of the apostles. They complained, "All these people are in the temple to hear Peter preach about Jesus? Those followers of Jesus are ignorant men, and have never studied the books of the Law like we have!"

"But nobody can deny that something has happened to these men," said one of the Sadducees. "Have you seen the miracles done in the name of Jesus?"

"Yes, it's amazing!" said another in the group. "They speak with authority, and we have seen how they have healed people in the name of Jesus Christ."

"It seems to me that you have started to believe all of this," shouted the High priest. "I don't care what good these men have done. I'm furious that they keep saying that Jesus rose from the dead! If they continue with that, they will convince everyone that Jesus is the Messiah."

Then they arrested the apostles and put them in the public jail. But that night, an angel of the Lord opened the prison doors and set them free, saying, "Go, stand in the temple courts and tell the people all about this new life."

The next day, when the high priest and his associates arrived at the temple,

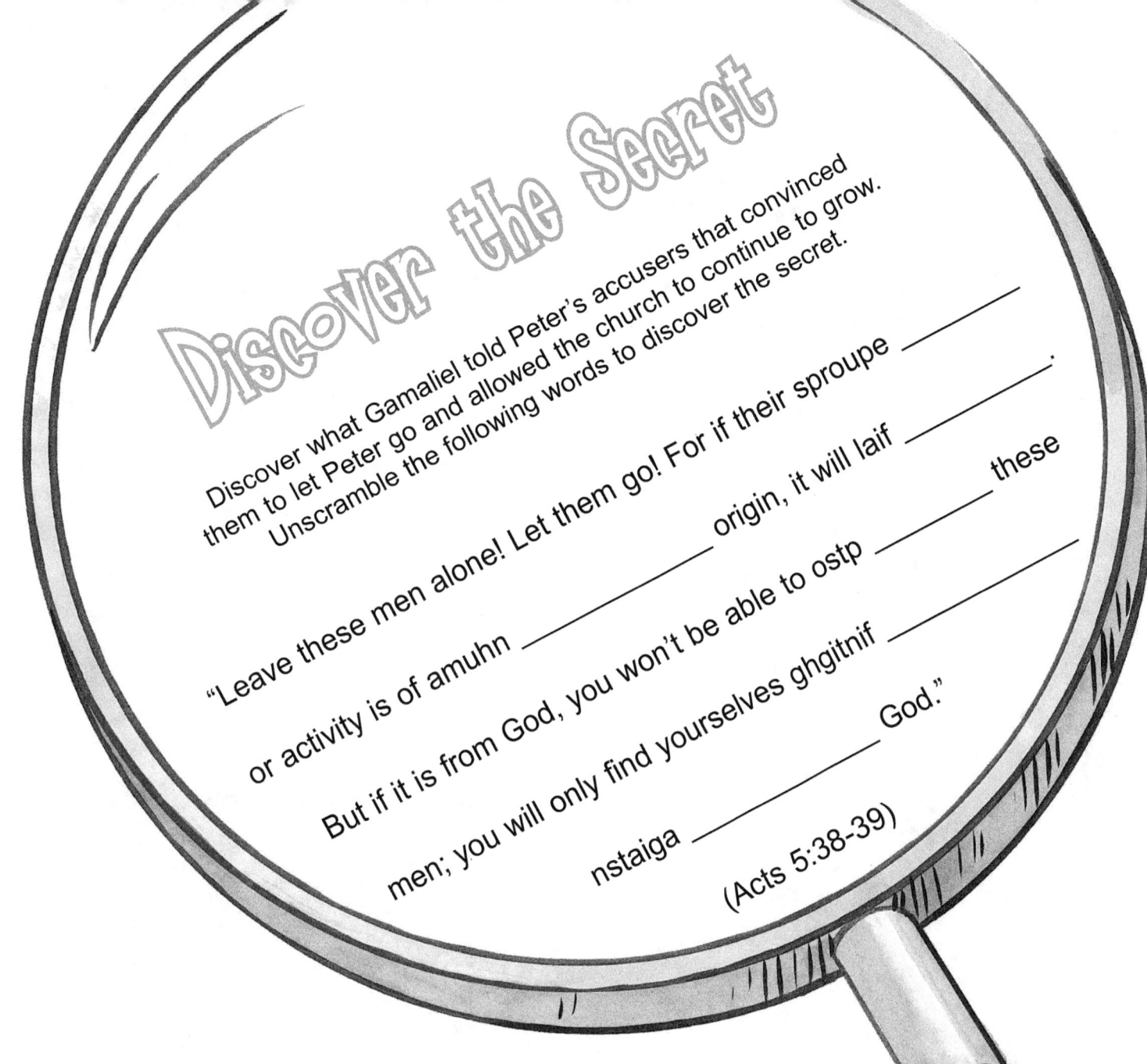

Discover the Secret

Discover what Gamaliel told Peter's accusers that convinced them to let Peter go and allowed the church to continue to grow. Unscramble the following words to discover the secret.

"Leave these men alone! Let them go! For if their sproupe _____ or activity is of amuhn _____ origin, it will laif _____. But if it is from God, you won't be able to ostp _____ these men; you will only find yourselves ghgitnif _____ nstaiga _____ God."

(Acts 5:38-39)

they summoned all of the Elders of Israel and ordered the guards, "Bring the prisoners for interrogation!"

When the guards found the prison cells securely locked and no one inside, they reported back to the assembly, "We found the jail securely locked, with the guards standing at the doors, but when we opened them, we found no one inside."

Then someone came and told them that the men who were put in jail were standing in the temple court teaching the people.

The high priest was furious. He said to the apostles, "You were warned to stop teaching about Jesus and have not obeyed our orders!" In response, they said, "We must obey God rather than men."

The members of the court were so angry that they wanted to kill the apostles. But Gamaliel, a beloved leader of the group, stood and said, "Leave these men alone! Let them go! For if their purpose or activity is of human origin, it will fail. But if it is from God, you won't be able to stop these men; you will only find yourselves fighting against God."

From Where Did Peter Get His Courage?

What do you think gave Peter the courage to face his persecutors?

Matthew 16:18
_____
_____
_____
_____
_____
_____
_____

Acts 1:8
_____
_____
_____
_____
_____
_____
_____

I Need Courage For...

Think about times when you will need courage to do something. Complete the following phrases:

I need courage to:
_____
_____
_____
_____
_____

I have courage knowing that:
_____
_____
_____
_____
_____

Have courage knowing that you are a Christian and you are part of the church of Christ.

Lesson 22

STUDENT WORKBOOK

A CHRISTIAN'S DUTY

Memory Verse: *"Then he said to his disciples, 'The harvest is plentiful but the workers are few. Ask the Lord of the harvest, therefore, to send out workers into his harvest field.' "* (Matthew 9:37-38)

The Lord's Workers

Place vowels (a, e, i, o, u) in the blank spaces to complete the words, and finish the Bible Verse - Matthew 9:37-38.

Th_n h_ s_ _d t_ h_s d_sc_pl_s, "Th_ h_rv_st _s pl_nt_f_l b_t th_ w_rk_rs _r_ f_w. _sk th_ L_rd _f th_ h_rv_st, th_r_f_r_, t_ s_nd _ _t w_rk_rs _nt_ h_s h_rv_st f_ _ld." Matthew 9:37-38.

Great Missionaries!

Mark the path of Barnabas and Paul on their first missionary journey. Acts 13:1-6.

Damascus

Jerusalem

Paphos   Antioch

Seleucia

Salamis

Judea

Cyprus

Samaria

89

Special Agents

Reporter 1: Paul and Barnabas I am so excited to meet you! Can you tell me what you did before becoming missionaries?

Paul: I'm ashamed to admit it, but my name was Saul and I hated Christians.

Reporter 2: Are you the same Saul who arrested and beat Christians?

Paul: Yes, I am….

Barnabas: Of course he is! It was very difficult for believers in Jerusalem to imagine Paul as a Christian. At first they thought it was a trick. And until I was sure he wasn't the same as before, I didn't take him to see the other Christians.

Reporter 1: How did you become missionaries?

Paul: Through God's command!

Reporter 2: What do you mean?

Paul: Let me explain. We were in Antioch worshiping with other believers when the Holy Spirit said, "Set apart for me Barnabas and Saul for the work to which I have called them."

Barnabas: There were many preachers and teachers in Antioch who laid their hands on us, prayed for us, and sent us out to share the gospel.

Reporter 2: You were called "special agents?"

Paul: I guess you could say that.

Barnabas: But that doesn't mean we're more important than other believers. God has given us all special assignments.

Reporter 1: I heard that you are called "the first missionaries." How did you know what you had to do?

Paul: Actually, we didn't know exactly what we were going to do. We just trusted and followed the mandate of the Holy Spirit.

Barnabas: When we went to a new city, we proclaimed the gospel in their synagogues. We told people that Jesus was the Messiah, the Savior of the world! Only he can forgive their sins and restore their lives.

Reporter 2: How did the people respond?

Paul (to Barnabas)**:** Barnabas, do we talk about Elymas and Sergius Paulus?

Barnabas: Sure.

Paul: We traveled across the island of Cyprus until we came to Paphos. The Roman governor Sergius Paulus lived there. He was an intelligent man because he wanted to hear the gospel message. I told him I was no longer Saul but Paul.

Barnabas: There we also met Elymas, the magician. He didn't want Sergius Paulus to listen to us, and tried to turn him from the faith. He didn't like what we had to say.

Reporter 2: What did you do?

Barnabas: The Holy Spirit gave Paul courage. He looked directly at Elymas and said, *"You are a child of the devil and an enemy of everything that is right! You are full of all kinds of deceit and trickery. Will you never stop perverting the right ways of the Lord? Now the hand of the Lord is against you. You are going to be blind for a time, not even able to see the light of the sun."*

Reporter 1: What a dreadful rebuke! What happened next?

Paul: Darkness fell upon him immediately and he went around looking for someone to lead him by the hand.

Reporter 2: Unbelievable!

Barnabas: Amazing! It is not very wise to fight against the Holy Spirit

Paul: That gave us the opportunity to teach Sergius Paulus about Jesus.

Reporter 1: What did the Governor think of all this?

Barnabas: *"When the proconsul saw what had happened, he believed, for he was amazed at the teaching about the Lord."*

Reporter 2: Imagine! The Roman Governor became a believer!

Reporter 1: What an exciting experience you had on your first missionary trip! I'm sure you have a lot more that you could tell us.

Paul and Barnabas: We sure do. But let's save that for another time. Thank you for allowing us to testify to you about what God did on our first missionary trip.

WHAT KIND OF A WITNESS ARE YOU?

Maybe you will never become a missionary like Paul and Barnabas, but you will always be a witness for Christ. People observe how you react when they oppose your faith. Read the following responses and tell in which situations a Christian could react this way.

Anger: Do you react violently when someone attacks you for what you believe?

Denial: Do you pretend, for the moment, NOT to be a Christian?

Courage: With a lot of courage, do you tell others that you love Jesus?

Verse of the Month Club

You can be a member of the Verse of the Month Club! Cut out the cards that have the Bible verse for each month printed on them. The verses are: Matthew 9:37-38, Luke 10:27 and Matthew 6: 9-13. These cards will help you memorize the verses.

You can get a star on your certificate as you learn the verses, one for each month. And on the last Sunday of the quarter, give your teacher the certificate so he/she can put the stars on for you.

Verse of the Month Club
Challenge

_____ is a member of the Verse of the Month Club.

_____
Teacher

☆ Month:_____   ☆ Month:_____   ☆ Month:_____

Then he said to his disciples, "The harvest is plentiful but the workers are few. Ask the Lord of the harvest, therefore, to send out workers into his harvest field." Matthew 9: 37-38

"He answered, 'Love the Lord your God with all your heart and with all your soul and with all your strength and with all your mind' and, 'Love your neighbor as yourself.'" Luke 10:27

"This, then, is how you should pray: 'Our Father in heaven, hallowed be your name, your kingdom come, your will be done, on earth as it is in heaven. Give us today our daily bread. And forgive us our debts, as we also have forgiven our debtors. And lead us not into temptation, but deliver us from the evil one.'" Matthew 6:9-13.

Lesson 23
Student Workbook

CHANGING PATHS

Memory Verse: "Then he said to his disciples, 'The harvest is plentiful but the workers are few. Ask the Lord of the harvest, therefore, to send out workers into his harvest field.'" (Matthew 9:37-38)

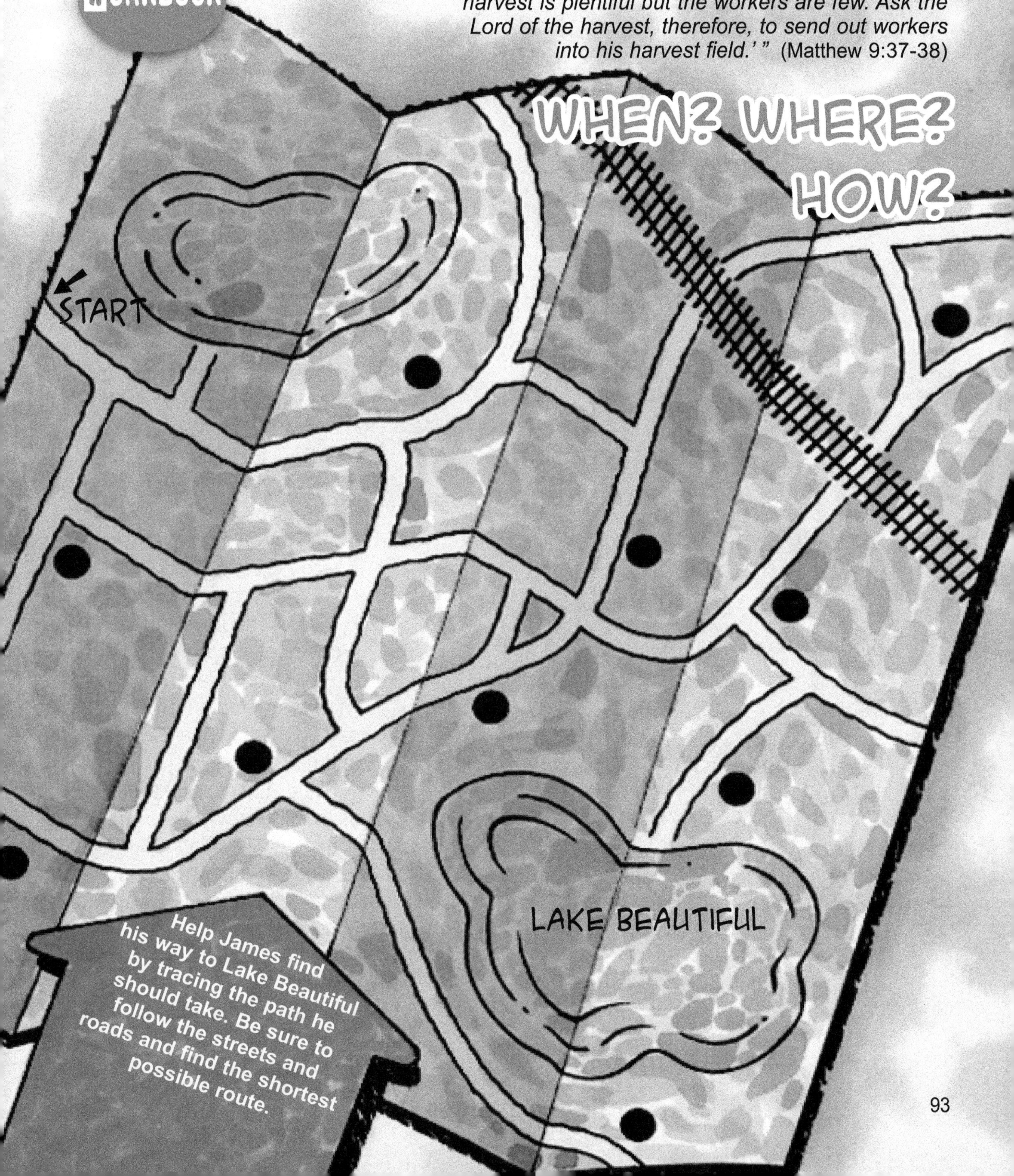

WHEN? WHERE? HOW?

START

LAKE BEAUTIFUL

Help James find his way to Lake Beautiful by tracing the path he should take. Be sure to follow the streets and roads and find the shortest possible route.

GOD DIRECTS THE PATH

"I wish I knew why the Holy Spirit didn't allow us to preach in Asia" said Paul.

"Maybe we should go anyway," said one of his companions. That seemed like a good idea to everyone and they began to make their way to that city. They tried to enter Bithynia, but the Spirit didn't allow it. Then they passed Mysia, and continued down to Troas.

Paul told Silas, "I'm tired. We should rest when we reach Troas."

"I'll be ready to rest then too," Silas agreed.

When they arrived at Troas, Silas, Timothy and Luke laid down to sleep.

That night, Paul had a vision: a man was standing, begging him saying, "Come over to Macedonia and help us."

"Silas! Luke! Wake up!" Paul exclaimed. "I know where God wants us to go."

While the others woke up, Paul explained his vision. "God wants us to go to Macedonia."

"Macedonia? But it's so far away!" someone said.

"Yes, Macedonia! In my vision I saw a man there. The man said, 'Come over to Macedonia and help us.'"

Paul and his friends packed up their things and went down to the port and arranged for their trip. When they arrived in Macedonia, the missionaries continued on to Philippi.

"Why did we come to Philippi?" It was the main city in that part of Macedonia. But there was no synagogue. "Why did the Holy Spirit bring us here?"

"How are we going to find people to talk to about Jesus if there isn't a synagogue?"

"We must start one!" Paul suggested, "Why don't we go outside the city? Many times when there isn't a synagogue, people meet at the river to pray. We should go to the river and see if anyone is there."

The missionaries didn't have to look for long. They quickly found a group of women who gathered there every Saturday to pray and encourage one another. Along the river, Paul, Silas, Timothy and Luke sat down and began to talk to the women about Jesus.

One of the women was named Lydia. She sold purple cloth. God had opened her heart so that she was attentive to Paul's message.

"I believe. I want to be Christian!" Lydia said.

Paul baptized Lydia and all of her household. Lydia was very happy because the missionaries had come to Macedonia. She invited them to her home. Then she said to them, "If you consider me a believer in the Lord, come and stay at my house."

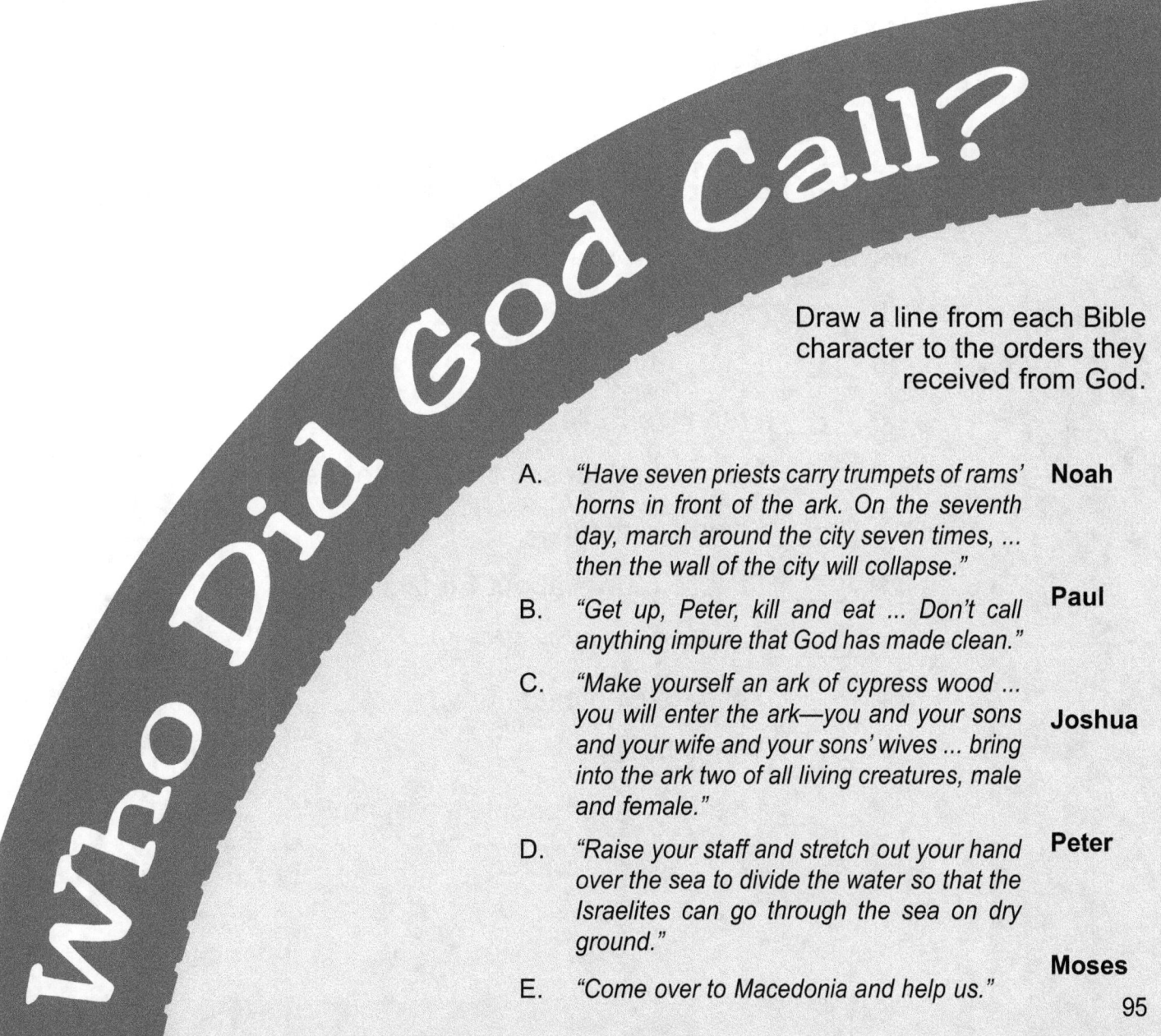

Who Did God Call?

Draw a line from each Bible character to the orders they received from God.

A. *"Have seven priests carry trumpets of rams' horns in front of the ark. On the seventh day, march around the city seven times, ... then the wall of the city will collapse."*

B. *"Get up, Peter, kill and eat ... Don't call anything impure that God has made clean."*

C. *"Make yourself an ark of cypress wood ... you will enter the ark—you and your sons and your wife and your sons' wives ... bring into the ark two of all living creatures, male and female."*

D. *"Raise your staff and stretch out your hand over the sea to divide the water so that the Israelites can go through the sea on dry ground."*

E. *"Come over to Macedonia and help us."*

Noah

Paul

Joshua

Peter

Moses

Lesson Review

Cross out the bold words that should not be part of the following sentences:

1. We were **allowed - forbidden** by the Holy Spirit to speak the gospel in Asia.

2. A man of Macedonia standing and begging Paul to go to Macedonia and **not help us - help us**.

3. After Paul had the vision, we got ready at once to leave for Macedonia, concluding that God **had - had not** called us to proclaim the gospel there.

Does It Please God?

Write YES or NO to indicate what does or does not please God.

a. _____ I tell a lie.

b. _____ I obey my parents.

c. _____ I read the Bible.

d. _____ I take what does not belong to me.

e. _____ I help the needy.

f. _____ I talk to others about Christ.

g. _____ I make fun of the elderly.

h. _____ I pray to God every day.

i. _____ I obey the law.

j. _____ I destroy other people's property.

Lesson 24

STUDENT WORKBOOK

GOD ACCEPTS US ALL

Memory Verse: *"Then he said to his disciples, 'The harvest is plentiful but the workers are few. Ask the Lord of the harvest, therefore, to send out workers into his harvest field.'"* (Matthew 9:37-38)

To An Unknown God

"Paul, are you sure you'll be fine here alone in Athens?" asked one of the men who accompanied him in Berea.

"I'll be fine, thanks," Paul replied. "Silas and Timothy will soon be here, anyway."

And so the men left. Paul began to observe the streets of Athens and the beautiful buildings. And as he looked around, his spirit became heavy seeing the city given over to idolatry. Every day he went to the synagogue and to the market to speak to the Jews and the Greeks.

In Athens, people were proud of their skills and knowledge. There were well-educated people who enjoyed going to public places and having conversations with well-prepared people.

Paul had a good education; he began teaching about Jesus and his resurrection. People from different groups gathered to listen. Some said, "What does he talk about?" and to others he seemed to be talking about a new god.

Soon, Paul's words caused a lot of curiosity among people and they said, "We want you to attend a meeting with our religious leaders, the most prepared. We'll meet at one of our temples." This meeting was called "the meeting of Aerópago." Paul was asked by the people, "Can we know about this new doctrine of which you speak? For you bring some strange things to our ears. We want to know what these things mean."

Paul stood and said, *"People of Athens! I see that in every way you are very religious. For as I walked around and looked carefully at your objects of worship, I even found an altar with this inscription: to an unknown god. So you are ignorant of the very thing you worship—and this is what I am going to proclaim to you."*

Then he told them, *"The God who made the world and everything in it is the Lord of heaven and earth and does not live in temples built by human hands. And he is not served by human hands, as if he needed anything. Rather, he himself gives everyone life and breath and everything else. From one man he made all the nations, that they should inhabit the whole earth; and he marked out their appointed times in history and the boundaries of their lands. God did this so that they would seek him and perhaps reach out for him and find him, though he is not far from any one of us."*

"Therefore, since we are God's offspring, we should not think that the divine being is like gold or silver or stone—an image made by human design and skill. In the past, God overlooked such ignorance, but now he commands all people everywhere to repent."

Then he told them the good news: that God sent Jesus to earth to be our savior. Jesus was crucified, but God raised him from death. This proves that Jesus is the Son of God. After Paul preached about Jesus' resurrection, some mocked his words. Others said, *"We want to hear you again on this subject."* Some believed and became followers of Jesus.

Yes, Paul, We Hear You!

Search your Bible for Acts 17:32-34 and find the three different reactions that people had when listening to Paul's sermon in Athens. Then write those reactions in the blank circles that appear below each of the drawings.

Write the letters that are not X's on the blank lines to discover what Paul announced to the people in Athens.

"TXhXeX GXoXdX wXhXoX mXaXdXeX tXhXeX wXoXrXlXdX aXnXdX eXvXeXrXyXtXhXiXnXgX iXnX iXtX iXsX tXhXeX LXoXrXdX oXfX hXeXaXvXeXnX aXnXdX eXaXrXtXhX . . . HXeX hXiXmXsXeXlXfX gXiXvXeXsX eXvXeXrXyXoXnXeX lXiXfXeX aXnXdX bXrXeXaXtXhX aXnXdX eXvXeXrXyXtXhXiXnXgX eXlXsXeX . . ."

A Letter from Paul

"Finally, a letter from my dear friend and teacher!" Timothy thought when he received Paul's letter. As he read it, he remembered the first time he heard Paul preach. Paul and Barnabas had come to Lystra, Timothy's birthplace.

At first, the citizens of Lystra treated Paul and Barnabas very well. But later they were angered by Paul's message. They stoned him and left him for dead. But it was through his preaching that Timothy and his mother and grandmother became Christians.

Timothy was very happy when Paul returned to Lystra for a second time. He was even happier when Paul chose him to be his assistant for the rest of his trip.

Paul and Timothy were the first Christians to go to Europe. Together they started churches in Philippi, Thessalonica and Berea. Memories flooded the mind of Timothy as he thought of how they had worked in the church at Ephesus. Now he was doing what Paul had assigned him to do. He was the pastor of the church in Ephesus. Lately, some false teachers had been creating many problems. Maybe Paul had something to tell him that would help, Timothy thought as he started reading.

To Timothy, my true son in the faith: Grace, mercy and peace from God our Father and Christ Jesus our Lord.

"As I urged you when I went to Macedonia, stay there in Ephesus so that you may command certain people not to teach false doctrines . . . The goal of this command is love, which comes from a pure heart and a good conscience and a sincere faith. Some have departed from these and have turned to meaningless talk. I thank Christ Jesus our Lord, who has given me strength, that

Paul's Plan

Paul gave Timothy five ways of being an example to others. Find them in the Bible story and write them on the fingers of the hand.

he considered me trustworthy, appointing me to his service. Even though I was once a blasphemer . . . I was shown mercy because I acted in ignorance and unbelief. The grace of our Lord was poured out on me abundantly, along with the faith and love that are in Christ Jesus."

"I am giving you this command in keeping with the prophecies once made about you, so that by recalling them, you may fight the battle well, holding on to faith and a good conscience."

"Don't let anyone look down on you because you are young, but set an example for the believers in speech, in conduct, in love, in faith and in purity."

Let your life, just as your words, be an example to others. Love like Jesus commands us to love, and be careful not to sin. Let your faith in Christ be known to all.

Don't neglect the gift that is in you, which was given to you by God. Timothy, you have been given gifts to build up the church. Meditate on these things; remain in them, that your progress may be seem by all. Take care of yourself and your doctrine, for in doing this you will save both yourself and those who hear you.

Paul, an apostle of Jesus Christ

A Letter To A Friend

Write a letter to a friend who is very dear to you. Testify that Christ is your Savior. Tell your friend that they can also be Jesus' friend if they will receive him into their heart as their personal Savior.

_____
_____
_____
_____
_____

Dear Timothy:

Search for the words hidden in the puzzle below.

```
L E T T E R O P Z
O S P E E C H A F
V L M G D F W U A
E Y O U T H J L I
L T I M O T H Y T
C O N D U C T M H
J E N E S M Q T U
```

LOVE
LETTER
CONDUCT
FAITH
YOUTH
PAUL
SPEECH
TIMOTHY

Lesson 26 STUDENT WORKBOOK

WHO IS MY NEIGHBOR?

Memory Verse: *"He answered, 'Love the Lord your God with all your heart and with all your soul and with all your strength and with all your mind'; and, 'Love your neighbor as yourself.'"* (Luke 10:27)

Who Is My Neighbor?

"Master, what must I do to inherit eternal life?"

The man who spoke to Jesus was an expert in religious law. He was testing him, trying to make him fall.

"What is written in the law?" said Jesus. "What do you read?"

This person cited the law. "Thou shalt love the Lord thy God with all your heart, with all your soul, with all your strength and with all your mind; and your neighbor as yourself."

"I already have it!" he thought. For years, people have argued about what the law means by using the word "neighbor." Some teachers would tell people to love your neighbor and hate your enemy.

He wanted to do what he thought was right, so he said to Jesus, "And who is my neighbor?"

The Lord was ready for this question and answered with a story:

"A man went down from Jerusalem to Jericho and fell among thieves, who stripped him, beat him and went away, leaving him half dead."

The expert knew that the road from Jerusalem to Jericho was dangerous. Thieves lived in the hills near the road and often attacked people.

Jesus continued, "It happened that a priest came down the road, and seeing the beaten man, passed on by. Likewise a Levite, upon seeing the man, passed by."

The expert continued to listen. He knew why the priest and the Levite had not stopped. The man could die while they were helping him, and the law said that the priests and Levites could not touch corpses. If they did, they were not allowed to work in the temple for some time.

Jesus continued the story. "But a Samaritan, as he journeyed, came to the place where the injured man was."

"A Samaritan!" he thought. "Everyone knows that the Samaritans are good for nothing."

Jesus continued, "When the Samaritan saw the poor man, he had compassion. He came and bound up his wounds, put him on his donkey, took him to an inn and took care of him."

The next day when he departed, he took out money for the inn keeper and said, "Take care of him, and whatever more you need as compensation, I'll repay you when I return."

Then Jesus looked at the expert and asked, "Who then of these three do you think was a neighbor to the man who was beaten and robbed?"

The expert said, "He who showed mercy on him."

Jesus said, "Go and do likewise."

Write in each heart the different ways in which you can show love to your neighbor.

Who Can I Share Jesus With?

We need to talk about Jesus to people. Write the missing letter in the blank spaces and you will find the name of the person who is your neighbor, and to whom you can talk about Christ.

(1) My Aunt's daughter

__ O __ S __ __

(2) Lives in the house that is next to mine

N __ __ G H __ __ __

(3) I learn from them at school

__ E __ __ H E __

(4) My Mom's brother

__ N __ L __

(5) My Mother's Spouse

__ __ T H __ __

(6) My Dad's sister

__ U __ T

The Lost Coin

"Look at that!" said one of the Pharisees, annoyed. "See how Jesus allows these tax collectors and sinners to gather around him? This man welcomes sinners and eats with them."

"How terrible!" said a scribe angrily.

Another Pharisee said, "If he really were a prophet or the Messiah, he would have nothing to do with such despicable people."

Jesus listened. He wanted to help them understand that he doesn't reject anyone and so he shared this parable:

"Suppose a woman has ten silver coins and loses one. Doesn't she light a lamp, sweep the house and search carefully until she finds it?"

The people thought, "It would be very sad to lose a coin of that value."

"I wonder if she planned to put it on a string with ten coins before marrying," another said.

(It was customary for women to wear a chain with ten coins on their head when they got married.)

"I hope to never lose a coin like that!" thought another.

"And when she finds it" Jesus continued, *"she calls her friends and neighbors together and says, 'Rejoice with me; I have found my lost coin.'"*

People could imagine friends and neighbors happily celebrating with her.

Jesus looked at the angry scribes and Pharisees and said, *"In the same way, I tell you, there is rejoicing in the presence of the angels of God over one sinner who repents."*

Lost!

Have you ever lost something that was valuable to you? Draw a picture of it and tell your classmates how you lost it and what happened next.

If it was so important or valuable to you, why did you lose it?

Reward

In the blank space below, write an announcement telling what kind of reward you would offer to someone who found your lost object.

God's Response

Answers the following questions according to today's Bible Story.

1. Who criticized Jesus?_____

2. Where did the coin get lost?_____

3. What did the woman do when she realized that she had lost her coin?_____
   _____

4. How did the woman feel when she found the lost coin?_____
   _____

With your teacher's guidance, discuss the following questions as a class.

   a. Do you think that God stops loving you when you are disobedient?

   b. What is sin?

   c. When you sin, are you close to God?

   d. Why do you think God seeks those who are sin?

   e. How does God feel when we repent of our sins?

   f. Why did Jesus compare the sinner with the lost coin?

Draw a picture of what you think happened in heaven when YOU asked God for forgiveness. Under your drawing write: **"I am valuable to God!"**

Lesson 28

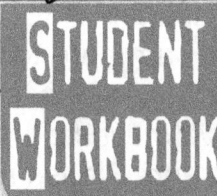

DON'T GIVE UP! KEEP TRUSTING!

Memory Verse: *"He answered, 'Love the Lord your God with all your heart and with all your soul and with all your strength and with all your mind' and, 'Love your neighbor as yourself.'"* (Luke 10:27)

OUR REQUESTS

What kind of prayers do people pray that they may not get the answer they want to?

Write an example on the hands.

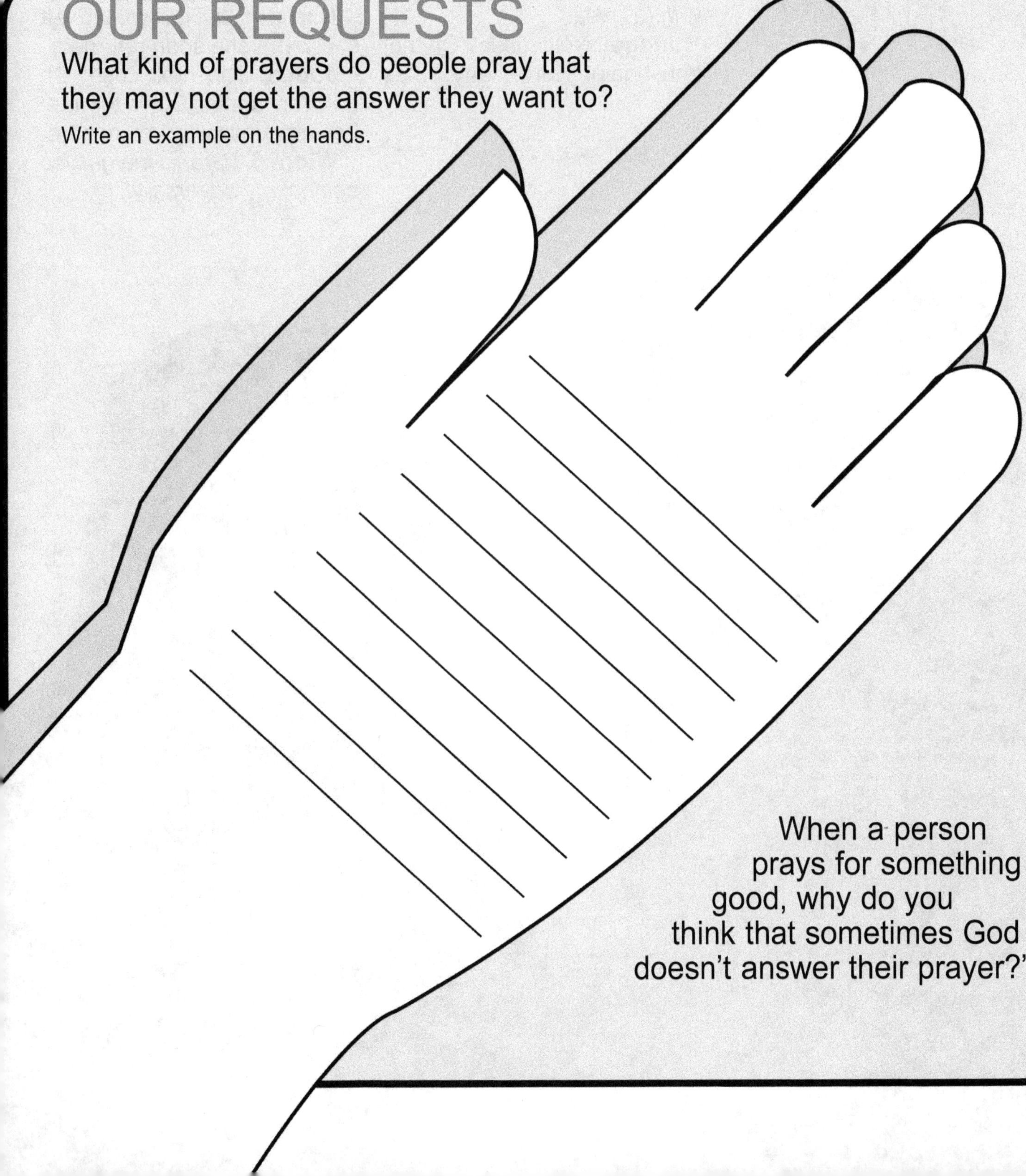

When a person prays for something good, why do you think that sometimes God doesn't answer their prayer?"

The Unjust Judge

Narrator 1: One day Jesus told his disciples a parable to showed them that they should always pray and not give up. He started by saying, "*In a certain town there was a judge who neither feared God nor cared what people thought. And there was a widow in that town who kept coming to him with* (a) *plea.*"

Judge: Next case! Oh no! You again! How many times have you come here? What do you want now?

Widow: I am here today for the same reason I came last time. *"Grant me justice against my adversary!"* Please resolve this conflict so that I can live in peace.

Judge: I'm still thinking. Now go. Leave me alone.

Narrator 2: The woman left sadly. But she soon returned.

Judge: The next case. Oh no! You again. Don't tell me. Let me guess why you're here.

Widow: *"Grant me justice against my adversary!"*

Narrator 1: For many days that followed, the widow returned to the judge.

Judge: What? You? Again?

Widow: "Grant me justice against my adversary!"

Narrator 2: For some time, the judge refused to do what the widow asked. But after a while, he said,

Judge: "Even though I don't fear God or care what people think, yet because this widow keeps bothering me, I'll see that she gets justice."

Narrator 1: It was not long until the widow returned to see the judge again.

Widow: "Grant me justice against my adversary!"

Judge: All right, you win! Now leave me alone!

Narrator 1: Then Jesus said to his disciples, *"Listen to what the unjust judge says. And won't God bring about justice for his chosen ones, who cry out to him day and night? Will he keep putting them off? I tell you, he will see that they get justice, and quickly."*

Judge the Judge

Rate the judge from the Bible story in each of the following categories. Draw an X on the line to show how you would rate him.

1. Did the judge know the facts of the case?
   _____
   a little knowledge / a fair amount of knowledge / full knowledge

2. Did the judge show signs of care and concern for the widow?
   _____
   no concern / a little concern / a lot of concern

3. Was he a fair judge?
   _____
   not at all fair / somewhat fair / very fair

What Kind of Judge is God?

Look up the following verses to find out:
The Knowledge of God: 1 Samuel 2:3; Psalm 44:21
God's Care: 1 Peter 5:7
God's Righteousness: 2 Timothy 4:8

Draw a star on the lines above to show what kind of judge God is.

What Did You Learn?

What have you learned from the parable Jesus told about the unjust judge?

- The Bible teaches that God listens to us no matter how many times we go to him.

- We can trust that God is fair and does the right thing.

- We cannot manipulate God to give us what we want.

- If even an unjust judge does good when we are persistent in asking, we don't have to worry about whether God will do good.

- We can trust that God will do the right thing, even if at times, it seems that he doesn't answer our prayers.

Lesson 29

STUDENT WORKBOOK

THE PARABLE OF THE SOWER

Memory Verse: *"He answered, 'Love the Lord your God with all your heart and with all your soul and with all your strength and with all your mind' and, 'Love your neighbor as yourself.' "*
(Luke 10:27)

What Difference Does The Soil Make?

Look at the two plants. Why do you think one is healthy and the other is dying? Cut out the lower left side of the page, up to the dotted line. Then fold the bottom of the page up along the dotted line and you will find what makes the difference. If it's hard for you, ask your teacher for help.

117

THE PARABLE OF THE SOWER

"A farmer went out to plant his field; some of his seeds fell on the road and the people who passed by stepped on them and the birds ate them. Other seeds fell where there were many stones; the plants sprouted, but soon died because they had no water. Others fell among thorns; the plants sprouted, but the thorns choked them and didn't let them grow. The rest of the seeds fell on good soil; the plants sprouted, grew and produced a crop that produced a hundred times more than what was planted."

"Look! Jesus is coming!" shouted a villager.

"And I see that some of our neighbors are already with him. Let's go so we can hear what he's saying."

Many villagers joined the crowd to hear the story Jesus was telling.

"A farmer went out to sow his seed," began Jesus. *"As he was scattering the seed, some fell along the path; it was trampled on, and the birds ate it up."*

The crowd looked at each other. Some of them were farmers and knew exactly what he was talking about, because this had happened in their fields.

"Some fell on rocky ground," Jesus continued, *"and when it came up, the plants withered because they had no moisture. Other seed fell among thorns, which grew up with it and choked the plants. Still other seed fell on good soil. It came up and yielded a crop, a hundred times more than was sown."*

"What does this parable mean?" the disciples asked.

"I am telling you some secrets about the kingdom of God," said Jesus. "You will understand, but some people will hear and won't know what it means."

"This story is like a riddle," they thought.

Later, Jesus' disciples asked him what the story meant, and so he said, *"This is the meaning of the parable: The seed is the Word of God. Those along the path are the ones who hear, and then the devil comes and takes away the Word from their hearts, so that they may not believe and be saved. Those on the rocky ground are the ones who receive the Word with joy when they hear it, but they have no root. They believe for a while, but in the time of testing they fall away. The seed that fell among thorns stands for those who hear, but as they go on their way they are choked by life's worries, riches and pleasures, and they don't mature."*

"Mmm," Murmured people. They had seen overgrown fields. Weeds don't let the seeds grow.

The disciples listened carefully until Jesus finished his explanation.

"But the seed on good soil stands for those with a noble and good heart, who hear the Word, retain it, and by persevering produce a crop."

What Do They Mean?

You have learned that a parable is a story that explains a difficult idea by comparing it to something common. Draw a line that links the symbols with their meanings.

1. Good Soil
2. Path
3. Seeds
4. Rocks
5. Thorns

A. People who hear the word, but the devil takes it away.
B. People who hear the word, but don't have any roots.
C. The Word of God
D. People who hear, but are choked by life's worries, riches and pleasures.
E. People who hear, remember it and preserver.

Lesson 30

IS IT BAD TO BE RICH?

Memory Verse: *"He answered, 'Love the Lord your God with all your heart and with all your soul and with all your strength and with all your mind' and, 'Love your neighbor as yourself.'"*

(Luke 10:27)

What opinion can people have of others just by looking at them? Pretend you are a detective; look at the drawings of the three children. What do you know about them just by looking at the pictures?

Seeing What's Important

If these children moved into your neighborhood, what would you like to know about them?

_____
_____
_____
_____
_____
_____
_____
_____

121

Lazarus and The Rich Man

"No servant can serve two masters," Jesus said. "You cannot serve both God and money."

The Pharisees, who loved money, sneered at him. "He wouldn't say that if he had money," the Pharisees thought. "Besides, our teachers taught us that God rewards those who serve him. Our money shows that God is blessing us. Jesus thinks God wants His chosen people to be poor? Everyone knows that being poor is a punishment from God."

"What people value highly is detestable in God's sight," Jesus said.

A disciple said, "You know how proud the Pharisees are of their wealth. They believe that large amounts of money show that God is pleased with them."

"There was a rich man who was dressed in purple and fine linen and lived in luxury every day," said Jesus. "At his gate was laid a beggar named Lazarus, covered with sores and longing to eat what fell from the rich man's table."

"What did the rich do to receive those blessings of God?" The Pharisees asked.

"I would like to know what Lazarus did to deserve such misery. I would not want to be him," thought another.

Jesus continued his story. "The time came when the beggar died and the angels carried him to Abraham's side.

The rich man also died and was buried."

"It probably was a glorious funeral!" thought the Pharisees. "But we are surprised that Lazarus was with Abraham. What is going on?" they asked.

Jesus continued. "In Hades, where he was in torment, he looked up and saw Abraham far away, with Lazarus by his side."

The Pharisees were amazed. "How could a beggar be with Abraham and a rich and blessed man be sent to hell?" This bothered the Pharisees.

Jesus continued telling his story. The rich man shouted, "Father Abraham, have pity on me and send Lazarus to dip the tip of his finger in water and cool my tongue, because I am in agony in this fire."

"But Abraham replied, 'Son, remember that in your lifetime you received your good things, while Lazarus received bad things, but now he is comforted here and you are in agony. And besides all that, between us and you a great chasm has been set in place, so that those who want to go from here to you cannot, nor can anyone cross over from there to us.'"

The rich man thought of his five brothers (who also had many possessions). "Then I beg you father, send Lazarus to my family, for I have five brothers. Let him warn them, so that they won't also come to this place of torment."

Who Said That?

"Father Abraham, have pity on me and send Lazarus to dip the tip of his finger in water and cool my tongue, because I am in agony in this fire." (Luke 16:24)

"Son, remember that in your lifetime you received your good things, while Lazarus received bad things, but now he is comforted here and you are in agony." (Luke 16:25)

"... covered with sores and longing to eat what fell from the rich man's table." (Luke 16:21a)

"... God knows your hearts. What people value highly is detestable in God's sight." (Luke 16:15b)

In this story, Jesus expresses some of the words that other Bible characters said. Look at the different verses to identify what words were said by which characters.

A SPECIAL VISION!

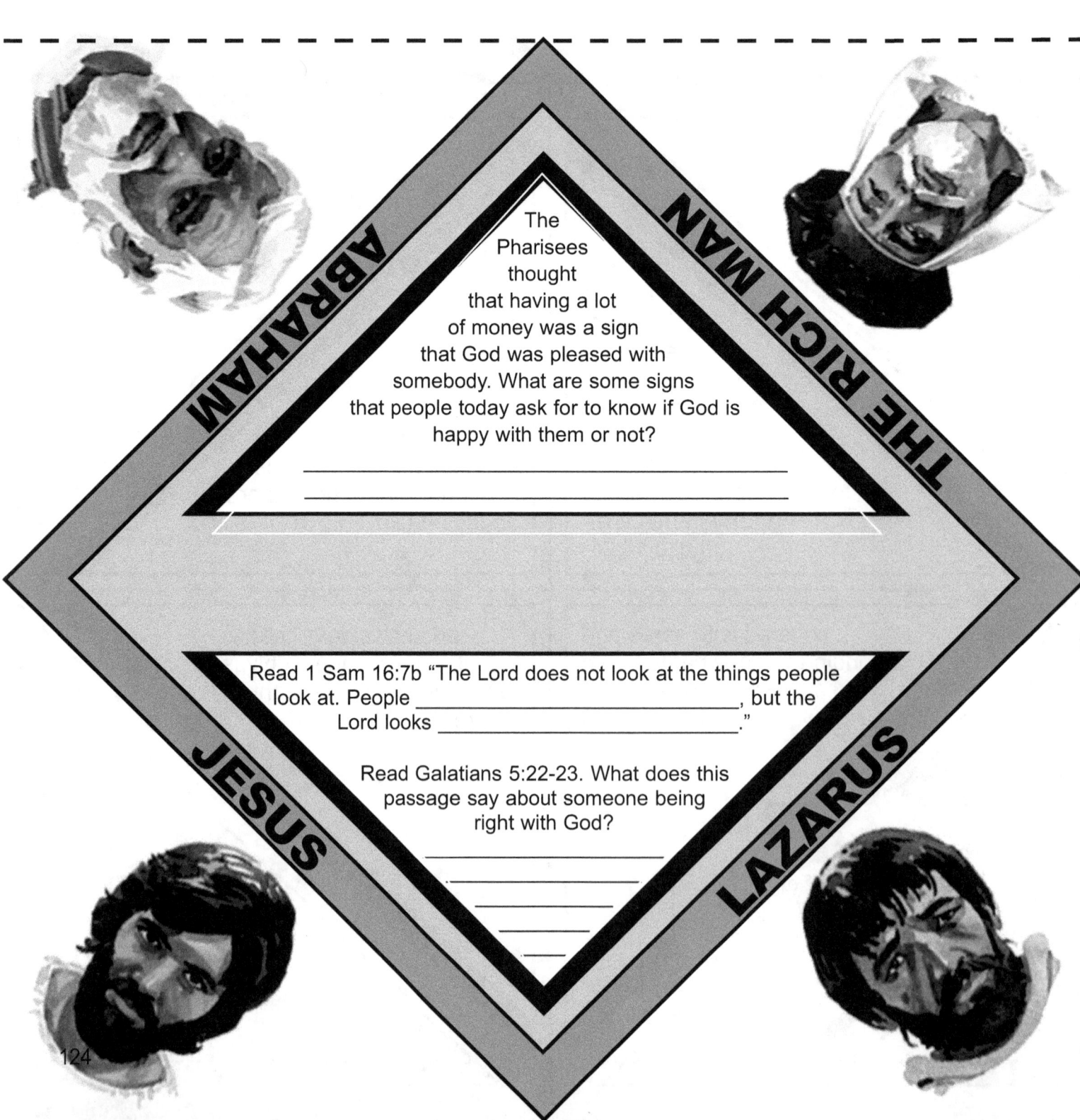

ABRAHAM — THE RICH MAN — JESUS — LAZARUS

The Pharisees thought that having a lot of money was a sign that God was pleased with somebody. What are some signs that people today ask for to know if God is happy with them or not?

_____
_____

Read 1 Sam 16:7b "The Lord does not look at the things people look at. People _____, but the Lord looks _____."

Read Galatians 5:22-23. What does this passage say about someone being right with God?

_____
_____
_____
_____

Lesson 31

STUDENT WORKBOOK

TO PRAY IS TO HONOR GOD

Memory Verse: "This, then, is how you should pray: 'Our Father in heaven, hallowed be your name, your kingdom come, your will be done, on earth as it is in heaven. Give us today our daily bread. And forgive us our debts, as we also have forgiven our debtors. And lead us not into temptation, but deliver us from the evil one.'" (Matthew 6:9-13)

An important part of life

What is happening in each photograph?

What do the photos have in common?

Why do you think they are doing these things?

Jesus teaches us to pray.

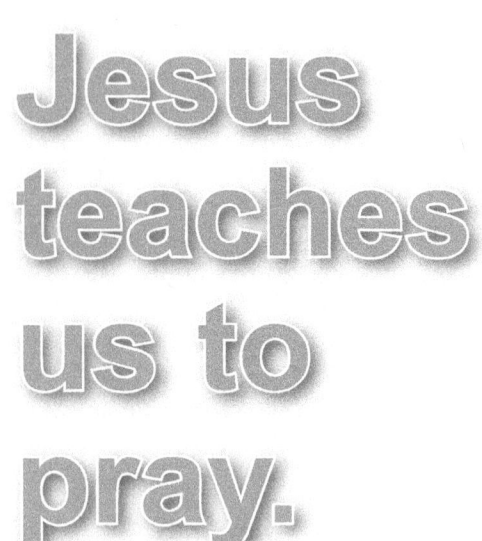

"Look back!" said one of the disciples to another one. "The crowd following Jesus is huge."

"Yes, the people have followed us everywhere we have been," said the other one.

Jesus wanted to get to a place where everybody would be able to hear his teachings, so he went up to the mountain and he sat and started to teach them. He loved to explain about God's Kingdom to people. He told them who would be blessed.

So Jesus said, "Don't think that I have come to abolish the Law or the Prophets; I have not come to abolish them but to fulfill them. For truly I tell you, until heaven and earth disappear, not the smallest letter, not the least stroke of a pen, will by any means disappear from the Law until everything is accomplished."

"The Pharisees would be glad to hear that," thought the disciples.

But Jesus had not finished. "For I tell you that unless your righteousness surpasses that of the Pharisees and the teachers of the law, you will certainly not enter the kingdom of heaven."

Some of the

people from the crowd were jabbing each other and raising their eyebrows. "How is that possible?" they asked themselves. "Pharisees keep more rules than everyone else!"

Jesus explained how love fulfills the law. Somebody who joined the crowd asked, "What did I miss?" "Jesus told us about everything," he was told, "murders, disagreements, about loving your enemies and helping the poor."

"When you pray, don't be as the hypocrites are," Jesus said, "for they love to pray standing in the synagogues and on the street corners, to be seen by others. If showing off is everything they want, truly I tell you, they have received their reward in full. But when you pray, go into your room, close the door and pray to your Father, who is unseen. Then your Father, who sees what is done in secret, will reward you. You don't have to worry about long and elaborate prayers. God is not impressed by many words. After all, your Father knows what things you have need of before you ask him.

This, then, is how you should pray. "Our Father in heaven, hallowed be your name, your kingdom come, your will be done, on earth as it is in heaven. Give us today our daily bread. And forgive us our debts, as we also have forgiven our debtors. And lead us not into temptation, but deliver us from the evil one. Amen." (Matthew 6:9-13)

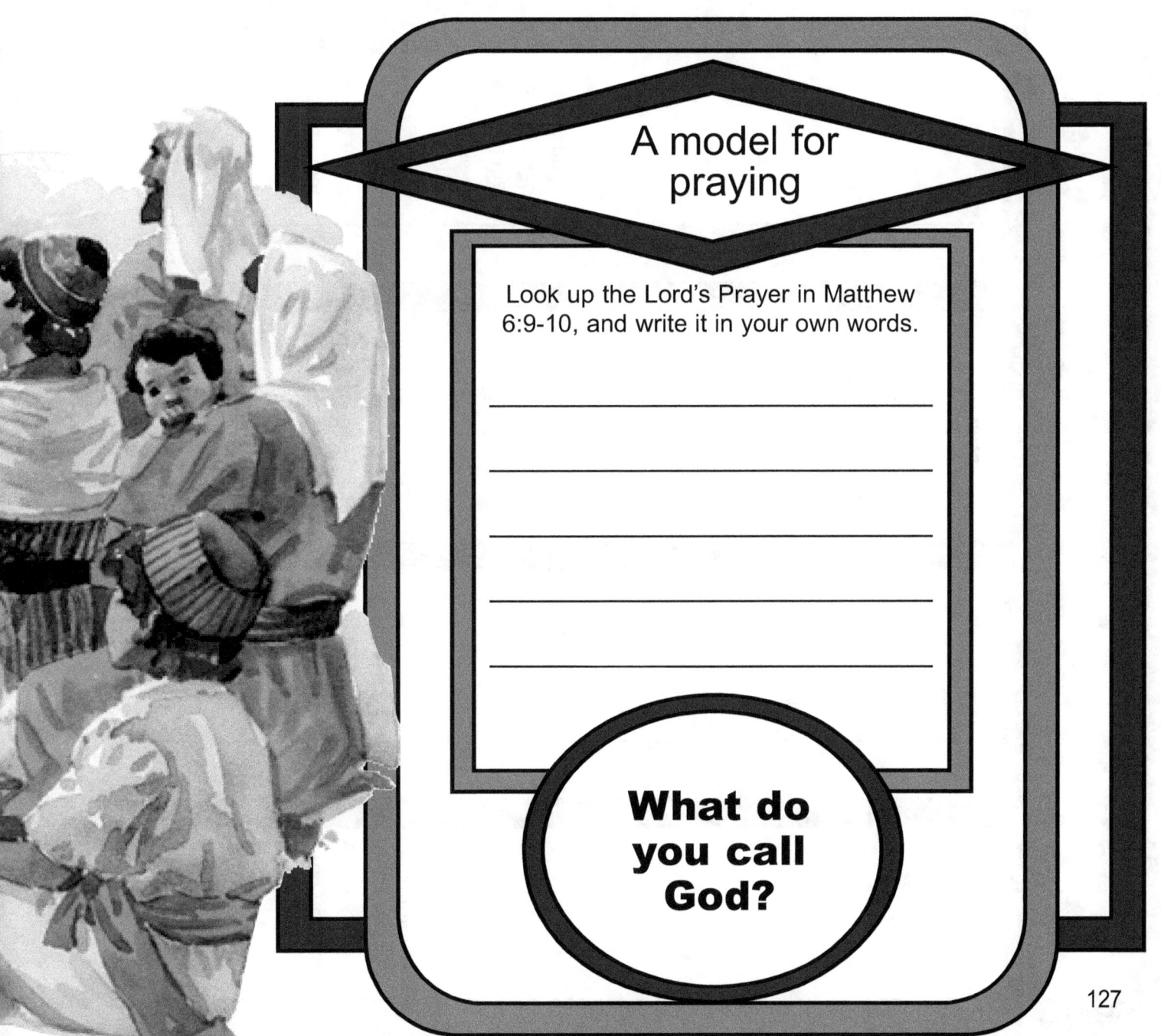

A model for praying

Look up the Lord's Prayer in Matthew 6:9-10, and write it in your own words.

_____

_____

_____

_____

_____

What do you call God?

STARTING YOUR PRAYERS WELL

1. What did Jesus mean when he taught us to call God "our Father who is in heaven"?

2. Read the definition of "sanctified":
- Make or keep something holy.
- Treat with respect
- Treat something with care because it belongs to God.

3. What does it mean that "God's will be done"? In what other prayer is it required that the will of God be done?

4. Why do you think Jesus taught that it is important to start our prayers by honoring God?

5. How did you honor God through your prayers last week?

6. How could you honor God through your prayers this week?

Lesson 32

TO PRAY IS TO PRESENT OUR NEEDS

Memory Verse: "This, then, is how you should pray: 'Our Father in heaven, hallowed be your name, your kingdom come, your will be done, on earth as it is in heaven. Give us today our daily bread. And forgive us our debts, as we also have forgiven our debtors. And lead us not into temptation, but deliver us from the evil one.' " (Matthew 6:9-13)

To whom does it matter?

Do you have any problems or needs? If so, write them on the packages in the basket that the boy is carrying. You can exchange your basket with a classmate and pray for each other during the week.

OUR DAILY BREAD

In the Lord's Prayer, we are taught to pray: "Give us this day our daily bread" (Matthew 6:11). What would be the other needs?

JESUS FEEDS THE 5000

"Have you heard the terrible news about John the Baptist?" asked one of the disciples with sadness on his face.

"Yes, we just heard about it," answered another disciple with a low voice.

"The dearest friend and cousin of Jesus ... dead! I can hardly believe it!"

"What did Jesus do when he heard the news?" asked another disciple.

"He went away in a boat."

"Did anybody go with him?"

"No, he wanted to find a quiet place where he could be alone. However after a little while, people started looking for Jesus. They wanted to bring their sick relatives and friends to Jesus to be healed and to hear his teachings."

"Do you know where Jesus is? My brother is very sick!" cried a man.

"He is there! Over in that boat!"

Jesus came to the bay and stopped his boat on the beach. When he got off his boat, he saw a huge crowd; he had compassion on them and healed those who were sick.

"I know that you can help me!" cried a woman.

"Jesus, come over here! Help me! Only you can do this," cried out another one.

The crowd surrounded Jesus. As soon as he touched someone, somebody else would call out his name.

"Please, Jesus! Help me!"

About dinner time, the disciples went to Jesus to tell him, "This place is deserted and it's getting late. Tell the people to go and look for food in the closest towns; they must be getting hungry."

"They don't need to go," Jesus said to his disciples. "You give them food."

The disciple couldn't believe what they were hearing. "How are we going to feed a huge crowd? There are at least five thousand men, plus women and children. We don't have enough money to buy food for all of them. And we only have two loaves of bread and five fish."

"Bring those to me," Jesus said.

The disciple gave Jesus the bread and the fish. Jesus told everybody to sit on the grass. Then he took the bread and fish, and raising his eyes to the heavens, he thanked God for the food. Then he divided the food into pieces, telling his disciples to start passing it out to the people.

Everybody ate and afterwards they picked up twelve full baskets of left overs.

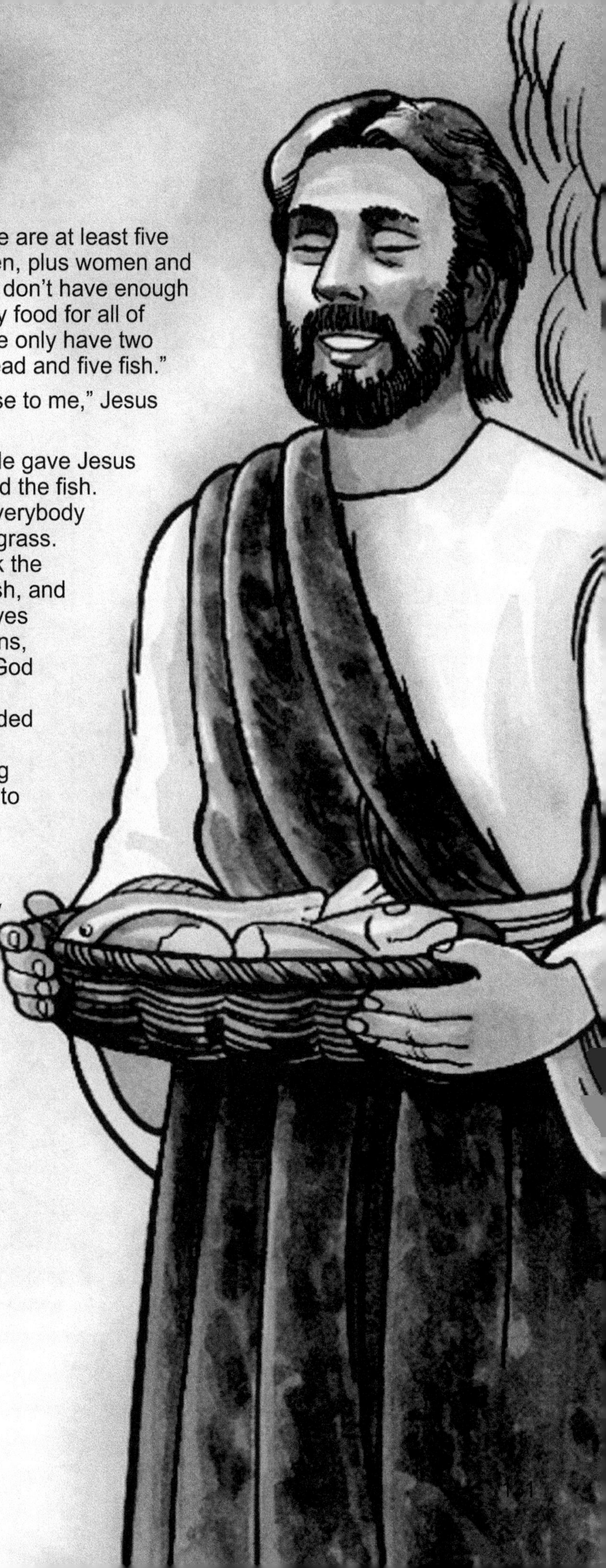

My Prayers

Circle what you have prayed for:

For someone we love who is sick.

 For a problem at school

For money

 For your church

For a friend who needs help

 For missionaries

For your family (make a drawing of your family below)

Lesson 33

STUDENT WORKBOOK

TO PRAY IS AN OPPORTUNITY TO FORGIVE AND ASK FOR FORGIVENESS

Memory Verse: "This, then, is how you should pray: 'Our Father in heaven, hallowed be your name, your kingdom come, your will be done, on earth as it is in heaven. Give us today our daily bread. And forgive us our debts, as we also have forgiven our debtors. And lead us not into temptation, but deliver us from the evil one.' " (Matthew 6:9-13)

The Right Help at the Right Time

Look closely at the drawings, and draw a line from the people who are in danger with the one that has the tool to help rescue them.

People who have acted badly also need to be forgiven. How can those who have acted badly find forgiveness?

As we forgive our debtors

In the Lord's Prayer that Jesus taught us to pray: "And forgive us our debts, as we also have forgiven our debtors" (Matthew 6:12).

Who is a debtor?

Can you think of someone whom you would call a debtor?

Are you a debtor to someone?

Write Matthew 6:12 in your own words.
_____
_____
_____
_____
_____
_____
_____
_____
_____
_____
_____
_____

The servant that didn't forgive

"Mom, how long do I have to forgive my brother?"

You're not the first to ask this. Did you know that Peter also did? He approached Jesus and asked him, "Lord, if a brother of the church does something against me, how often should I forgive him? Up to seven times?" Jesus answered, "I tell you, not seven times, but seventy times seven." We must forgive again and again; that is, forever. And for the disciples to understand this better, Jesus told them a parable:

"The kingdom of God works like something that happened some time ago in a far away country. A king summoned his employees to inform them what they owed him. When he started checking accounts, he saw an employee who owed him a lot of money. Since the employee didn't have any money to pay his debt, the king ordered him to be sold as a slave, along with his wife and children, and also to sell everything he had. This was so he could start paying back the debt with the money made.

But the employee knelt before the king and begged,

"Lord, have patience with me and I'll pay you everything." The king felt sorry for his employee and said, "Go quietly. I forgive you all that you owe me."

Leaving the palace of the king, that employee met a fellow who owed him 100 silver coins. He grabbed him by the neck and said, "Pay me back what you owe me."

This fellow knelt before him and begged, "Give me a little more time and I'll pay you!" But he refused and put him in jail until he paid the money he owed. Another fellow, seeing what had happened, went to tell the king. Then the king asked to see the evil employee and said,

"How wicked you are! I forgave all that you owed me because you begged me. Why didn't you have mercy on the other man as I had on you?"

The king was furious and ordered that the employee be punished until he paid all that was due.

Jesus concluded, "So will my Father in heaven deal with each of you unless you forgive your brother sincerely."

DID YOU FORGIVE?

The disciples understood how they should forgive. We are studying the Lord's Prayer to also learn how to pray. One part says, "Forgive us our debts as we forgive our debtors." Do you think the servant's attitude was wrong? Of course it was! Because he was forgiven his debt, the Lord expected him to be able to forgive the one who owed him.

Answer the following questions:

Have you ever asked for forgiveness? _____
_____

Have you ever forgiven someone? _____
_____

Has someone ever asked you to forgive them for something they did?
_____

Have you forgiven them? _____

The Lord Jesus Christ forgives you of your sins, but also expects you to forgive those who offend you. If you have a friend who is angry at you, go and ask them for forgiveness. You will see that you'll feel much better when you don't have problems with anyone. And if someone comes to you to ask for forgiveness, remember not to reject them, because Jesus forgives you and you should do the same for others if you want to go to heaven.

Lesson 34

TO PRAY IS A WAY TO ASK FOR PROTECTION

Memory Verse: "This, then, is how you should pray: 'Our Father in heaven, hallowed be your name, your kingdom come, your will be done, on earth as it is in heaven. Give us today our daily bread. And forgive us our debts, as we also have forgiven our debtors. And lead us not into temptation, but deliver us from the evil one.' " (Matthew 6:9-13)

What do all the objects in each category have in common? Write your answers in the spaces.

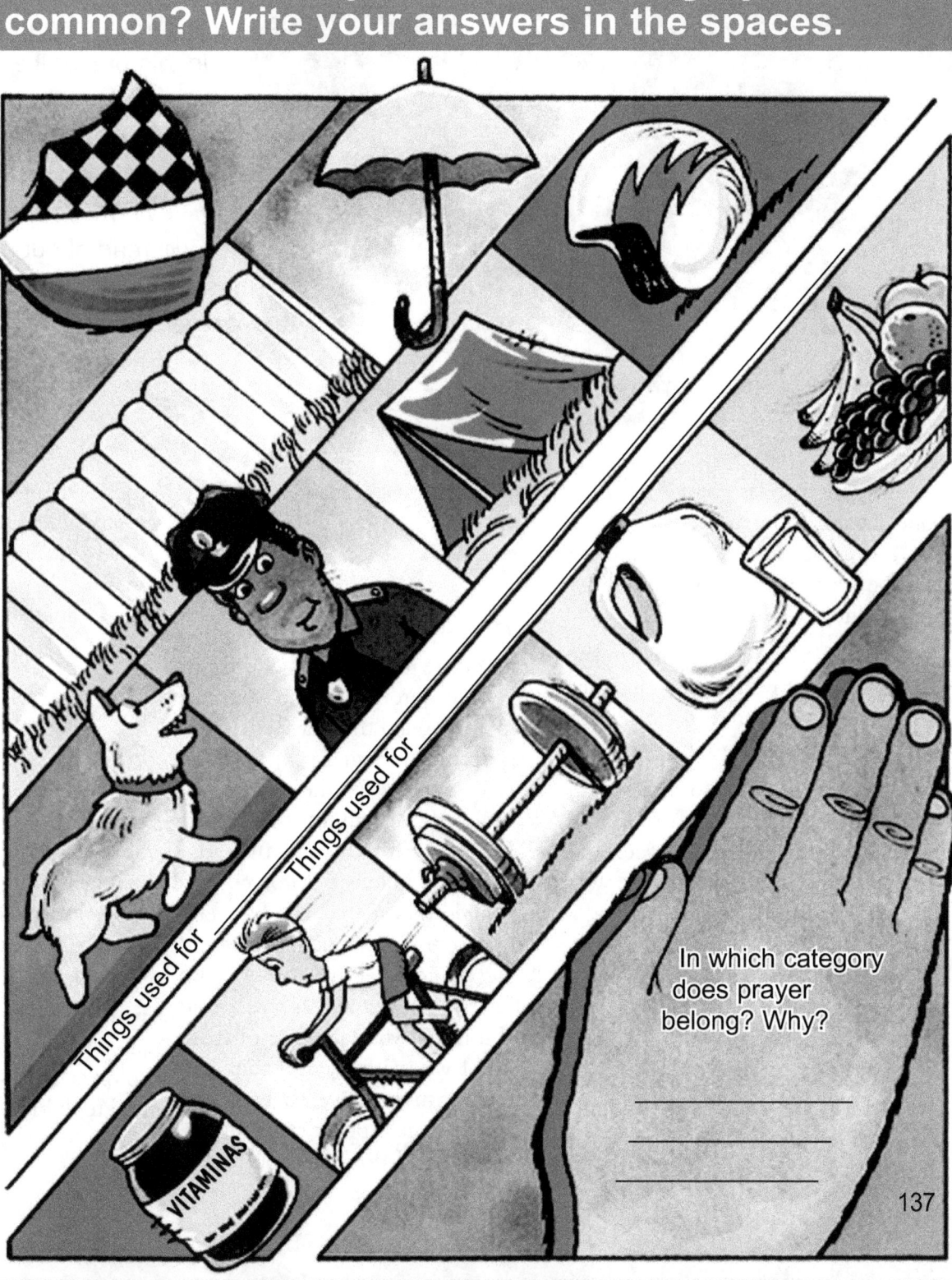

Our Best Defense

Things used for _____

Things used for _____

In which category does prayer belong? Why?

_____
_____
_____

A comparison

In the Lord's Prayer we are taught to pray like this: "Don't lead us into temptation, but deliver us from evil" (Matthew 6:13). Was Jesus asking God to keep Christians from hearing or seeing the evil of this world?

Does it mean that Jesus implied in this prayer that Christians would never be affected by evil or by what evil people do?

What does "deliver us from evil" mean? In today's story you will read about another time when Jesus prayed. How similar are these two prayers?

JESUS PRAYS FOR HIS DISCIPLES

"Where is Judas going?" asked one disciple to the other.

"Since he handles our money, maybe he is running an errand for Jesus" said the second disciple.

After Judas left, Jesus spoke to the disciples about what they would face in the future. He predicted his death and spoke about his resurrection.

"I've said all this so you would not stop trusting in me. You will be expelled from the synagogue, and the day will come when anyone who kills you will think he's doing God a favor."

Then Jesus began to pray, saying, "My Father, the time has come for you to show people how powerful I am. Thus, I also have shown them how great and wonderful you are. To everyone I showed how great and powerful you are, because I did everything you commanded me."

"Why does this prayer sound like his last?" some asked.

The disciples heard Jesus talking to God about them. "I have shown who you are to the followers you gave me. They were yours, and you gave them to me, and they have obeyed all I commanded them. I pray for them. I'm not praying for the people who don't accept me and just think about the things of this world. Instead, I pray for the followers who you gave me and they're yours. Heavenly Father, soon I won't be in the world, because I go where you are. But my followers will remain in this world. So I ask that you take care of them. While I was with them, I took care of them with the power that you gave me, and none stopped trusting me except Judas. I don't ask you to take them out of the world but that you protect them from Satan. I am not of this world, and neither are they. Your message is true; help them to listen and surrender completely to you."

The disciples thought about Jesus' words: "I don't pray only for them but also for those who will believe in me when they hear your message."

They must have thought to themselves, "I wonder how many will believe us if Jesus is not here?!" "Who will believe in our message? Not the religious leaders who are here!"

"Shortly after Jesus said this prayer, he and his disciples left the place where they had been. They went to an olive orchard. There, a band of soldiers led by Judas arrested Jesus and took him away."

When I pray...

When I pray, I feel happy knowing that God provides what I need.

When I pray, I give thanks to God for everything, for my food that I eat and for the songs that I sing.

When I pray, I ask God with love to help my grandfather who is in pain.

When I pray, I ask the Lord to help me love him with all my heart.

When I pray with all my heart, I give thanks to God for his compassion.

GOD'S PROTECTION

Think of some of the situations in which you have felt God's special protection. Write about one of those situations or tell someone about that time.

Write a prayer of thanksgiving for God's protection.

_____

_____

_____

Remember the four lessons in which we have talked about prayer. Don't forget to write down some personal prayer requests. Have you received an answer from God about one of your prayer requests? If so, write it down here as well.

_____

_____

_____

_____

Lesson 35

STUDENT WORKBOOK

DAVID, THE VICTORIOUS KING

Memory Verse: "It is the Lord your God you must follow, and him you must revere. Keep his commands and obey him; serve him and hold fast to him." (Deuteronomy 13:4)

Recipe for a great leader

Which characteristics do you think one must have to be a great leader? What would you like your leader to be like? Make a recipe for the leader that you would want to have. If you want, you can share your recipe with others in the class.

Recipe for a great leader:
_____
_____
_____
_____
_____
_____
_____

David's Secret strategy

""King Saul is dead!" shouted the people of Judah.

Then the general of Saul's army made his son, Ish-Bosheth, king over Israel.

When Saul's son died, the leaders of Israel came to David and made him king. The people had a new king; but not everyone was happy with the news.

"Now is the time to attack Israel," Israel's enemies, the Philistines, said.

A general told his king, "Israel is weak, but David becomes more powerful every day." So the Philistines all went up to capture him.

Upon learning this, David went down to the fortress in search of a safe and quiet place; he needed time to meditate and pray.

He knew he had to make a decision. The question was, what should he do?

And David inquired of the LORD, "Shall I go against the Philistines in battle? Will you deliver them into my hands?" God said to him, "Go, for I'll surely deliver the Philistines into your hands."

The victory was so fast that the Philistines fled without even stopping to get their idols. However, they didn't give up, but gathered in the valley of Rephaim to make a new plan of attack.

But David again went to God to ask what he should do. Then, the Lord gave David a secret plan for the war: "Don't go straight up to fight them, but circle around behind them and attack them in front of the poplar trees. As soon as you hear the sound of marching, move quickly, because that will mean the Lord has gone out in front of you to strike the Philistine army."

David did exactly as God commanded. He and his soldiers waited quietly near the trees. And when they heard the noise of their marching, they attacked.

(2 Samuel 5)

SECRET STRATEGY

The Bible tells us about the secret strategy that David used to be a good king and win the battles. Decipher the secret message using the following code.

Accept G O D A S Y O U R
L E A D E R.

Ask F O R G O D ' S
G U I D A N C E.

F O L L O W G O D ' S
guidance.

Code
1 A, 2 C, 3 D, 4 E, 5 I, 6 U, 7 L, 8 M, 9 N, 10 O, 11 P, 12 R, 13 S, 14 T, 15 F, 16 W, 17 Y, 18 G

MY SECRET STRATEGY

When you have to make a difficult decision, how will you decide what to do?

_____

_____

You can continue being a member of the Verse of the Month Club.

The verses to memorize are:
- Month .... Deuteronomy 13:4
- Month .... Luke 6:27-28
- Month .... Galatians 6:10.

Get a star added to your certificate when you have memorized the corresponding verse.

Verse of the Month Club

You can continue being a member of the Verse of the Month Club. Cut out the cards below that have the scripture verses printed on them in order to study each verse better. At the end of each month, get a star on the certificate, as long as you have learned the text well and memorized it.

"It is the Lord your God you must follow, and him you must revere. Keep his commands and obey him; serve him and hold fast to him." (Deuteronomy 13:4)

"Love your enemies, do good to those who hate you, bless those who curse you, pray for those who mistreat you. (Luke 6:27-28)

"Therefore, as we have opportunity, let us do good to all people, especially to those who belong to the family of believers." (Galatians 6:10)

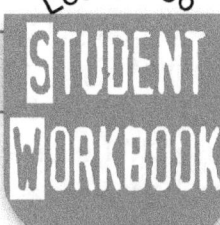

Lesson 36 — STUDENT WORKBOOK

WHEN GOD SAYS "NO"

Memory Verse: "It is the Lord your God you must follow, and him you must revere. Keep his commands and obey him; serve him and hold fast to him." (Deuteronomy 13:4)

THE BIG "NO"

Most people don't like the word "NO." Are you one of them? What do you think these kids are thinking?

The one who said "no" to the king

"At last there is peace in my kingdom," King David thought. "The army of Israel has defeated the Philistines, and they won't bother us for a while. Now I can enjoy my beautiful palace."

One day, Nathan the prophet visited King David and the king said to him, "Look, I live in a cedar house, while the Ark of God is in a tent. It doesn't seem right. I think I'll build a beautiful place for God.

"Do all that is in your heart, for the Lord is with you," answered Nathan.

"I'll have to make plans," David said.

But that night, the word of the Lord came to Nathan, and he immediately went to speak with David to communicate the message of God.

"God has given me a message for you, David," Nathan told him. "Thus says the LORD, 'Shall you build me a house where I'll dwell? I have never lived in a house from the day that I brought the children of Israel out of Egypt to this day, but walked in the tent and in the tabernacle. Did I ever ask you to build me a house?'"

"God favors you, David," Nathan continued, "but he wants it to be one of your children and not you that builds a house for him." After the prophet Nathan left, David prayed,

"You have become great, O Lord God, because there is none like you, and there is no God beside you. I wanted to build this house for you, but you have said that it won't be me who does it. O sovereign Lord, you are God."

Why does God say "NO"?

Read scenes 1 and 2 and then discuss the questions below that are highlighted in yellow.

Scene 1

Characters: Matias, Sergio and Leonel.
 These three friends meet at school during lunch time.

Matias: What do you think about Sunday school?
Sergio: It's AWESOME! I love what we learn from the Bible in every class.
Matias: Hey! I didn't know that God says "no" to important people like David. I thought He would only be saying "no" just to kids like us.
Leonel: Yes, but what was wrong with wanting to build a temple for God?
Matias: That's not the point, Leonel.
Sergio: God often says "yes." But when he says "no," it is for some reason.
Matthias: Of course, even if we don't know that reason, God is sovereign. This means that He doesn't have to tell us why He says "yes" or "no."
Leonel: I thought that God says "no" to prevent us from getting into trouble, like the Commandments that keep us from doing evil.

David wanted to do something good for God. Why do you think God commanded him to not build the temple?

Why didn't David ask God why?

Do you think that God still says "no" today?

Scene 2

Characters: Diana, Elizabeth and Liliana
 The three girls meet in a house to do their homework. While Elizabeth and Liliana study, Diana sighs deeply and looks very sad.

Elizabeth: Diana, is something wrong?
Diana: Today I had a terrible day. I got a bad grade on my exam and I don't understand why.
Liliana: Maybe some of your answers were wrong.
Diana: Very funny! I know that my answers were wrong, but I thought that God would help me.
Liliana: What do you mean?
Diana: I knew we were going to have a test. I even took the books to my house to study. The problem was that I was watching a TV show...
Elizabeth: So you didn't study enough?
Diana: Well ... no. But when I went to school I started praying before I started the exam!

Why do you think God didn't help Diana get a good grade?

What would you say to her if she asked you why God didn't help her?

Read the Memory Verse for this lesson, define the key words, and then put the letter of the correct answer in the blank space.

1. ___ **Follow:** a) Do what you want when you want to. b) Go behind, to imitate. c) Do the opposite of what you want to do.

2. ___ **Revere:** a) Look to God with love and respect. b) Consider yourself more important than others. c) Impress someone.

3. ___ **Commands:** a) Rules to obey when you have problems. b) Directions that you must follow. c) Directions that only adults must obey.

4. ___ **Obey:** a) Don't listen to what someone says. b) Follow and do what God tells us each day.

5. ___ **Serve:** a) Ask questions. b) Work for someone.

6. ___ **Hold fast:** a) Make something go fast. b) Not let go of or leave someone. c) To glue something.

Lesson 37 — Student Workbook

IN SEARCH OF WISDOM FROM GOD

Memory Verse: "It is the Lord your God you must follow, and him you must revere. Keep his commands and obey him; serve him and hold fast to him." (Deuteronomy 13:4)

What I want most in *the world*

Professor Amanda had completed a research project, and arranged each of her notes in order. It began with the most popular answers, then the least likely ones. But her dog knocked them out of her hands and they were all mixed up. Do you want to help the teacher get them back in order? They can go it in the following way: number them from 1 to 11, with 1 being the most popular choice given by most people, then the less popular ones, and so on until all of them are completed.

____ Money
____ Intelligence
____ Games/toys
____ Popularity
____ Fame
____ Wisdom
____ Health
____ Good at sports
____ Power
____ Strength
____ Great life

149

A Wise Decision

Narrator: Solomon, the son of David, became king of Israel at the age of twenty. One night God appeared to him in a dream and said to him, "Ask me what you want me to give you."

Solomon: Since I am very young and don't know how to solve problems, grant your servant an understanding heart to judge your people and to discern between good and bad.

Narrator: People soon realized how much wisdom Solomon had. Many came to him to solve their problems.

Soldier: Salute King Solomon! Hail, O king Solomon, the wisest man in all the earth!

Solomon: Who came to see me today?

Soldier: Two women, my lord.

Solomon: Let them come!

1st woman: Ah, my Lord! This woman and I live in the same house, and I gave birth while I was with her in the house. It happened that on the third day of giving birth, she gave birth to her son too. One night, this woman's son died because she laid on him. She got up at midnight and took my son from my side while I was sleeping. She put him next to her and placed her dead son beside me.

2nd woman: No! That is not true, my son is the one who lives and her son is the one who has died!

1st woman: No, your son is the dead one and my son lives!

Solomon: Soldier, bring me a sword.

Narrator: Suddenly, there was great silence. How would King Solomon decide the truth?

Solomon: Cut the living child in two, and give half to one, and half to the other.

1st woman: No, my Lord! Give the living child to her and don't kill him.

2nd woman: Neither I nor you will have it, cut it in half!

Solomon: Deliver the living child to the first woman, and don't kill him; She is his mother.

Narrator: All Israel heard the judgment that the king had pronounced, and they revered him, because they saw that God had given him wisdom to judge. (From 1 Kings 3)

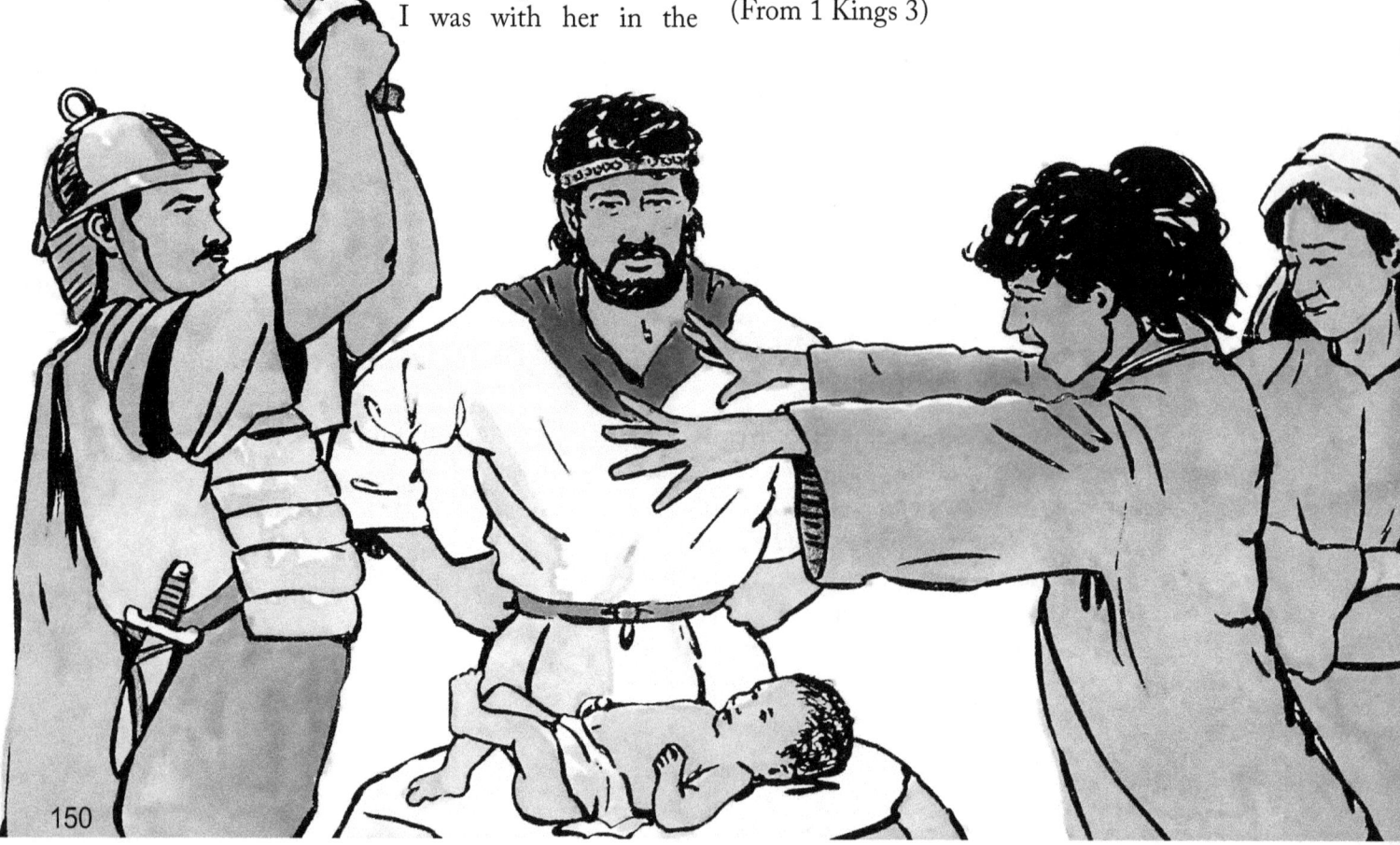

LIKE THE SAND OF THE SEA

"God gave Solomon wisdom and very great insight, and a breadth of understanding as measureless as the sand on the seashore."
1 Kings 4:29.

Solomon wrote proverbs, and many of them can be found in the book of Proverbs. Use your wisdom to know what to do in each of the following situations in which you could find yourself. Look up the Biblical passages that you will find below, and write in the blank spaces the Proverb that you think applies to that particular situation.

Difficult situations

____ 1. While you and a friend are buying things at the supermarket, your friend wants to steal something and asks you if he can hide it in your backpack.

____ 2. Some of your friends say bad words because it makes them feel bigger and stronger. Do you want to be like them?

____ 3. Andrew tells you that he has a really big problem and you cannot tell anyone. Later you tell him a secret and he tells others. Now, you want to tell others about the problem that he confided in you about.

____ 4. You have a problem at home with one of your brothers, and you want to take revenge against him, although others have counselled you not to do it.

____ 5. At school there are many kids who make fun of the kids who wear worn out clothes. Will you make fun of them as well?

THE WISDOM OF SOLOMON

A. "A gossip betrays a confidence, but a trustworthy person keeps a secret." (Proverbs 11:13)

B. "Keep your mouth free of perversity; keep corrupt talk far from your lips." (Proverbs 4:24)

C. "The way of fools seems right to them, but the wise listen to advice." (Proverbs 12:15)

D. "Whoever mocks the poor shows contempt for their Maker; whoever gloats over disaster won't go unpunished." (Proverbs 17:50)

E. "Don't set foot on the path of the wicked or walk in the way of evildoers." (Proverbs 4:14)

WISDOM, where does it come from?

Find the Bible references from Proverbs that are hidden among all the things.

- 2:6 – "For the Lord gives wisdom; from his mouth come knowledge and understanding."
- 9:10 – "The fear of the Lord is the beginning of wisdom, and knowledge of the Holy One is understanding."
- 10:23 – "A fool finds pleasure in wicked schemes, but a person of understanding delights in wisdom."
- 15:33 – "Wisdom's instruction is to fear the Lord, and humility comes before honor."

Lesson 38

STUDENT WORKBOOK

SOLOMON GIVES HIS BEST

Memory Verse: "It is the Lord your God you must follow, and him you must revere. Keep his commands and obey him; serve him and hold fast to him." (Deuteronomy 13:4)

The Great Project

"David has crowned his son Solomon to be the king of Israel," King Hiram of Tire said. "He and I are good friends. I'll send a message welcoming Solomon."

When Solomon received the message from this king, he was very happy to know that he wanted to be friends with the people of Israel. "We can help each other," he thought.

Solomon also sent a message to Hiram. "You know that my father David couldn't build a house in the name of the Lord his God because of the wars in which he was wrapped up in, until the Lord put his enemies under his control. Now, the Lord my God has given me peace everywhere. I, therefore, have determined to build a house in the name of the Lord my God, according to what the Lord said to my father David, 'Your son, whom I'll place on the throne after you, will build a house for my Name.' I want to use cedar wood from Lebanon for the temple," continued Solomon.

"Please have your men cut the trees. I'll pay whatever wages you say. My men will help, but as you know, we have no one who knows how to cut wood like your men."

Then the king of Tire answered Solomon's message. "My men will cut down all the cedar and cypress you need," said Hiram. "They will carry the wood to the sea, tie them together to form rafts, and then they will transport them by sailing them to the place where you want them. There you will separate them and thus you will be able to take them to your palace. In payment, you will give me food for my house."

So Hiram sent Solomon the cedar and cypress wood for the temple. As payment, he gave the king of Tire thousands of barrels of wheat and gallons of olive oil for food. So did Solomon and Hiram for many years.

Solomon also needed stones for the foundations of the temple. So, he sent 70,000 haulers, 80,000 rock cutters and 3,300 supervisors to the mountains. These men cut and removed large rocks to make the foundation, worked the wood, and prepared the rocks for the construction. Other workers did the interior finishing of the temple. For seven years, these people worked to build a house for God. When at last they were finished, Solomon gathered all the leaders of Israel. "Now is the time to bring the ark of Jehovah," he told them.

The priests carried the ark of the covenant of the Lord to a special place in the temple, the most holy place. The cherubim covered the ark with their outstretched wings. Inside the ark there were the two tablets of the law (10 Commandments), which Moses had placed inside at Horeb, where God made a covenant with the Israelites after they had left Egypt.

When the priests came out of the holy place, a cloud filled the temple of the Lord. They could not finish the service because the cloud prevented it. The glory of the Lord filled everything with his presence. This cloud was the symbol of the Lord's presence in his temple.

Solomon said, "The LORD has said that he will dwell in the darkness, but I have built Him a house to be in, a place where he can dwell forever."

Then he turned to the people and said, "Blessed be the Lord, the God of Israel, who has promised to David my father what he has done with his hand."

(From 1 Kings 5 and 8)

MY GIFTS TO GOD

How beautiful these gifts are! Would you like to give them to God? Then make a list of everything that you will give Him, and then write them on each of the boxes.

Lesson 39

STUDENT WORKBOOK

SOLOMON TURNED AWAY FROM GOD

Memory Verse: "It is the Lord your God you must follow, and him you must revere. Keep his commands and obey him; serve him and hold fast to him." (Deuteronomy 13:4)

DANGER IN SIGHT!

What are the objects that you can see in the drawing that could be dangerous to the boat? He should be careful of the rocks and the waves.

Now think of situations or problems that are dangerous for Christians, and write them on the rocks and on the waves.

157

Problems in the Palace

"Is it true what we have heard from Solomon?" asked many people. "Is he as wise and rich as they say?"

From all parts of the world, people came to visit King Solomon: kings, queens, important people ... they all sought his advice, and he answered questions no one else could. But after he became very famous, he began to forget God's commands. He married foreign women, not caring that his heart started leaning towards their foreign gods. Solomon was not obedient to God. He made deals with foreign kings, he agreed to marry their daughters, and he ended up doing so with seven hundred wives and three hundred concubines (those who didn't belong to royalty or had great titles).

When Solomon was old, his wives convinced him to worship pagan gods. In order to please his wives, he ordered places to be built to offer sacrifices to those gods.

Solomon did evil in the sight of the Lord. Unlike his father David, he was not obedient to God. The Lord was angry because Solomon's heart had departed from him. On two occasions, the Lord appeared to him to tell him not to worship other gods, but he was disobedient and ignored God's warning.

And God said to Solomon, "Because you have done this, and have not kept my covenant and the statutes which I commanded you, I'll take away all the kingdom, and will give it to your servant. However, I won't do it while you are alive. For your father David's sake, I'll take it out of your son's hand."

The peace that prevailed among the people no longer existed. Other nations began to oppose Solomon. Even his own men turned against him, and one of them was Jeroboam.

Solomon had put him in charge of the workers who worked on the project to repair the walls around the city. One day as Jeroboam came out of Jerusalem, the prophet Ahijah found him on the road. He was covered with a new cloak, and they were alone in the field. The prophet took the cloak, cut it into twelve pieces, and said to Jeroboam, "Take ten pieces for you, for thus says the Lord, the God of Israel, 'I'll tear the kingdom out of Solomon's hands and give you ten tribes. He will keep a tribe for my servant David's sake and for Jerusalem's sake. I do this because he has left me and worshiped other gods, and has not walked in my ways to do what is right in front of my eyes and my statutes. You will be king of Israel if you listen to all that I command you, walking in my ways and doing what is right before my eyes, keeping my statutes, as my servant David did. I will be with you.' "

When Solomon heard what had happened, he tried to kill Jeroboam, but Jeroboam fled to Egypt and remained there until Solomon's death. Then Jeroboam returned to Israel.

When the Israelites heard that Jeroboam had returned, they proclaimed him their king. Only the tribe of Judah remained faithful to Rehoboam, the son of Solomon. Rehoboam gathered a great army of Judah to fight against Jeroboam, because he wanted to recover the territory that had belonged to his father Solomon and which Jeroboam now ruled.

And the LORD spoke to Shemaiah the man of God, saying, "Speak to Rehoboam, and say to him, 'This is what the LORD says. Don't go out to fight against your brothers, the children of Israel. Everyone should return to their own house, because this is my work.' " When they heard the words of God, everyone returned to his house according to what the Lord had said to them.

The reign of Solomon ended after forty years. His kingdom was divided and they didn't enjoy peace. Now his son Rehoboam didn't have a great kingdom to lead. If only Solomon had remembered the proverb he wrote: "The faithful man will receive many blessings." (Proverbs 28:20)

(1 Kings 11 & 12)

Don't ignore God's warnings

Margaret received Jesus as her Savior when she was in the third grade at school. She read her Bible, prayed, went to church and used her talents for God.

When she reached the sixth grade, her new neighbor Michael moved next door. She thought that if she tried to become his friend she could talk about the Bible, church activities and Jesus. But Margaret began to listen to Michael's ideas, telling her that church was only for adults, and she began to believe this. She stopped praying, and read her Bible only when she went to church. And she began to do all the bad things Michael advised her.

What happened to Margaret and why?

What do you think of what she did?

Michael became more important for her than God. Even when she attended church on Sundays, she didn't worship or love the Lord. When the time came to attend high school, Margarita and Michael ended up going to different schools.

In English class, Margaret saw some of the classmates she had met in church camp as a child. They were Christians. One afternoon, they invited her to hang out with them and she agreed to go with them. She noticed how they treated each other and her. She thought how different they turned out to be.

How did her new friends make her feel?

Why were they different from Margaret?

Lesson 40

FACING A CHALLENGE

Memory Verse: "Love your enemies, do good to those who hate you, bless those who curse you, pray for those who mistreat you." (Luke 6:27-28)

THE WORRIED ONES

People care a lot about themselves, whether it is something small or big. Write your concerns on the shirts of the pictures of "the worried ones."

161

DON'T WORRY!

"Therefore I say to you; Don't be anxious about your life, what you will eat or what you will drink; or about your body, or what you will wear," Jesus said.

The disciples looked at each other. "Don't worry?" they thought. "We have lots of reasons to worry. We gave up work to follow Him! Our families need food, clothing and a place to live. Who will take care of them while we are following Jesus?"

The Lord clearly knew what his disciples were concerned about when he spoke to them. But he wanted them to know that they could trust that he would take care of them and their families.

Jesus continued with his sermon: "Is not life more than food, and the body more than clothes? Look at the birds of the air; they don't sow or reap or store away in barns, and yet your heavenly Father feeds them. Are you not much more valuable than they? Can any one of you by worrying add a single hour to your life? And why do you worry about clothes? See how the flowers of the field grow. They don't labor or spin. Yet I tell you that not even Solomon in all his splendor was dressed like one of these. If that is how God clothes the grass of the field, which is here today and tomorrow is thrown into the fire, will he not much more clothe you—you of little faith?"

"So don't worry, saying, 'What shall we eat?' or 'What shall we drink?' or 'What shall we wear?' For the pagans run after all these things, and your heavenly Father knows that you need them. But seek first his kingdom and his righteousness, and all these things will be given to you as well. Therefore don't worry about tomorrow, for tomorrow will worry about itself. Each day has enough trouble of its own."

Years later, Paul became a follower of Jesus' teachings. While in prison, he wrote a letter to his friends in Philippi. He didn't know if he would get out of that place alive, but he wanted his friends to trust in God no matter what happened.

"I know what it is to be in need, and I know what it is to have plenty," Paul wrote in his letter. "I have learned the secret of being content in any and every situation, whether well fed or hungry, whether living in plenty or in want. My God will meet all your needs according to the riches of his glory in Christ Jesus."

(From Matthew 6 and Philippians 4.)

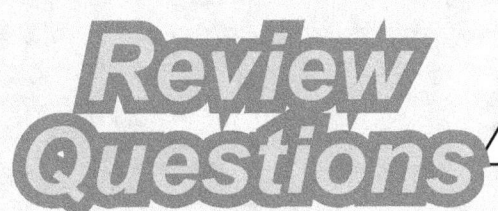

Answer the following questions from the lesson:

1. What did Jesus tell the people they shouldn't do?
   _____

2. What worried the disciples?
   _____
   _____
   _____

3. Jesus said that the disciples had little ......
   _____

4. What did Jesus tell the Disciples they should look for?
   _____

5. Where was Paul when he wrote the letter to his friends in Philippi?
   _____

6. What did Paul what his friends to know?
   _____
   _____
   _____

Treasure Chest

Write in the treasure chest of the world what you think won't be in heaven, and write in the treasure chest of God, what you think will be in heaven.

Be a winner!

What is something that worries you? Think about what it is and talk with God about it.

Lesson 41

STUDENT WORKBOOK

LOVING THOSE WHO DON'T LOVE US

Memory Verse: "Love your enemies, do good to those who hate you, bless those who curse you, pray for those who mistreat you." (Luke 6:27-28)

Would you love someone like this?

Why do you think these people are being sought? Think about it and write it on the line below the drawings in the blank space. Then draw in the blank box who you consider to be your enemy. (Don't mention names of real people.)

Wanted: Peter the dangerous for
_____
_____

Wanted: The grumpy neighbor for
_____
_____

Wanted: Fighting friends who
_____
_____

_____
_____
_____

A contrary Answer

While Jesus went around preaching and healing to the people, some religious leaders didn't agree with what He spoke about or what He did. They became his enemies and plotted to kill him.

One night, Jesus went to the Garden of Gethsemane to pray; when he returned, he found his disciples sleeping.

"Are you still sleeping? Look, they come, and the Son of Man is delivered into the hands of sinners. Rise! Let us go! Here comes my betrayer!" said Jesus.

Suddenly, lots of people with spears and sticks appeared. Judas came close to Jesus and said, "Greetings, Rabbi!" Then he gave him a kiss on the cheek, the same way that friends greeted each other in those days. This was the signal that Judas said would show which one was Jesus. How terrible that one of the disciples had become His enemy.

But Jesus said to him, "Do what you came for, friend."

Then the men surrounded Jesus and arrested him. His other disciples couldn't believe what was happening and wanted to defend him. Peter even took out his sword and cut off the ear of the servant of the high priest. This wasn't what Jesus had wanted to happen. He knew his mission, he knew that they would arrest him and then crucify him, but he also wanted to protect his disciples.

"Put your sword back in its place," Jesus said to him, "for all who draw the sword will die by the sword. Do you think I cannot call on my Father, and he will at once put at my disposal more than twelve legions of angels? But how then would the Scriptures be fulfilled that say it must happen in this way?"

After all of this, Jesus did something surprising: he touched the ear of the high priest's servant and healed it. Afterwards he said to his enemies, "Am I leading a rebellion, that you have come with swords and clubs? Every day I was with you in the temple courts, and you didn't lay a hand on me. But this is your hour – when darkness reigns."

All of His disciples fled in fear for their lives, leaving him alone. Later, they understood what Jesus wanted to say that night when he said, "Love your enemies" (Matthew 5, 26; Luke 22).

What does that mean?

"But I tell you, love your enemies and pray for those who persecute you." Matthew 5:44.

Enemy: A person, group or country that has bad desires and attitudes towards the other, and that continuously wants and seeks its evil.

Mercy: Compassion that drives one to help or forgive. Doing good to an enemy, doing that which is better than is expected.

BIBLE COMMENTARY
For Students

In Matthew 5:38-48, Jesus teaches us to love our enemies. If we love God and understand His love towards others, we can experience this type of caring for others.

"What kind of love does God talk to us about?" It's not only a feeling, it's an action. It's not to say that our enemies will begin to like us, but at least we can forgive those who have hurt us. In order to love in this way, it is necessary to use the power of God. We can suffer when we love like this, but our love towards others shouldn't change; this is the kind of love that pleases God. It's quite possible that our enemies won't change, and perhaps we won't get their love in exchange, however you are obeying God's wishes.

TELEPHONE MESSAGE

Using the numbers found on the telephone keys as a code, write the corresponding letter in the blanks above each number, and the words will be formed. When finished, you'll find a verse from Luke 6:27-28. Some words are already written as an example.

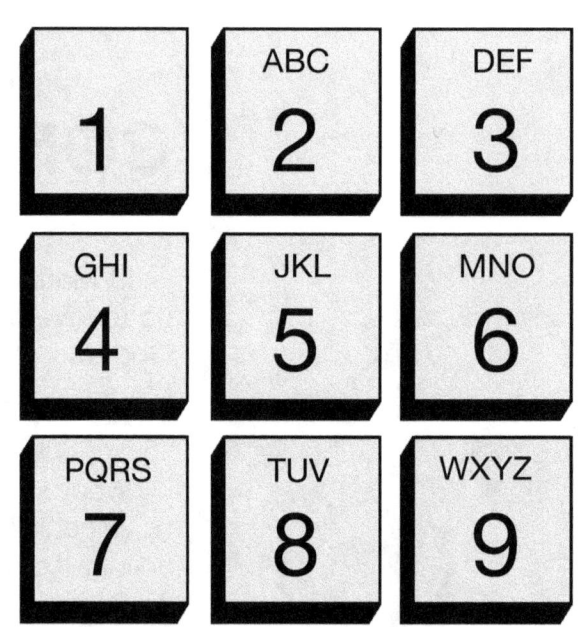

LOVE Y O U R   E N E M I E S, D O GOOD T O   T H O S E
5 6 8 3   9 6 8 7   3 6 3 6 4 3 7   3 6   4 6 6 3   8 6   8 4 6 7 3

W H O   H A T E   Y O U, BLESS THOSE W H O   C U R S E
9 4 6   4 2 8 3   9 6 8   2 5 3 7 7 8 4 6 7 3   9 4 6   2 8 7 7 3

Y O U, P R A Y   F O R   T H O S E   W H O   M I S T R E A T
9 6 8   7 7 2 9   3 6 7   8 4 6 7 3   9 4 6   6 4 7 8 7 3 2 8

YOU.
9 6 8

Lesson 42 — Student Workbook

THE MERCY OF JESUS

Memory Verse: "Love your enemies, do good to those who hate you, bless those who curse you, pray for those who mistreat you." (Luke 6:27-28)

Who is who?

Draw a line from the person to the award that they won.

169

Jesus went through the grain fields on the Sabbath. His disciples were hungry and began to pick some heads of grain and eat them. When the Pharisees, who had been following Jesus and spying on him, saw this, they said to him, "Look! Your disciples are doing what is unlawful on the Sabbath." Jesus knew that the Pharisees didn't care that the disciples were hungry. They didn't feel love nor did they care very much about circumstances; the only thing they cared about was carrying out the law and the authority that that gave them.

Jesus reminded them of the story of David when he was escaping from King Saul: "Haven't you read what David did when he and his companions were hungry? He entered the house of God, and he and his companions ate the consecrated bread – which was not lawful for them to

The disciples were hungry

do, but only for the priests. Or haven't you read in the Law how the priests desecrated the temple on the Sabbath and yet were innocent? If you had known what these words mean, 'I desire mercy, not sacrifice,' you would not have condemned the innocent. For the Son of Man is Lord of the Sabbath."

The Pharisees stopped their discussion with Jesus, but He knew they hadn't changed their way of thinking; they would keep trying to find faults with Jesus and try to find a way to destroy him.

(Matthew 7 and 12)

What it means

"Don't judge, or you too will be judged. For in the same way you judge others, you will be judged, and with the measure you use, it will be measured to you."
(Matthew 7:1-2)

Condemn:
  a. To say that a person or something is wrong.
  b. To accuse, to blame.
  c. To punish or sentence.

Judge:
  a. A person that has enough knowledge to give an opinion of something
  b. To blame or critique.
  c. To think or suppose something.

BIBLICAL COMMENTARY FOR STUDENTS

Matthew 7:1-5

Jesus mentions something very important: "Don't judge, or you too will be judged." The key to understanding what Jesus said is in his words: "For in the same way you judge others, you will be judged, and with the measure you use, it will be measured to you." Verse 2 says that people will judge. The important thing is the types of judgments that people make.

Jesus taught us to treat others the same way we want them to treat us. If someone harshly judges others, the same will be done to them. That doesn't mean that people can write their own rules. It means that we shouldn't look for the faults of others. How can we avoid judging others as Jesus warned?

Remember that God forgave us when we didn't deserve it. He sent Jesus to save us, not to condemn us. God is good and helps those in need. He is a forgiving God. Be wise in making decisions.

Remember, the way that you judge others will be the way they judge you.

Write a Telegram!

Give thanks to God for having sent his Son Jesus Christ to save us.

Lesson 43

STUDENT WORKBOOK

FOLLOWING JESUS' STEPS

Memory Verse: *"Love your enemies, do good to those who hate you, bless those who curse you, pray for those who mistreat you."* (Luke 6:27-28)

SIGNS

Do you always like people telling you what to do?

Do you know a child or person that doesn't obey the rules and just does what they want?

Look at the signs on this page. What would happen if people ignored them?

Is it safe?

Jesus had dedicated many hours teaching His disciples and the rest of the people who would listen to him. He told them not to worry about their food or clothing. He reminded them that God loved them all and would supply their every need.

He also told them to love their enemies; for if they only loved the people that loved them, they weren't any better than the people who didn't love God.

He also told them not to judge others unfairly. He reminded them that they should take a look at their own wrong doings before telling others about theirs.

Jesus knew that people forgot his teachings easily. Because of this, he told them this story:

"Therefore everyone who hears these words of mine and puts them into practice is like a wise man who built his house on the rock. The rain came down, the streams rose, and the winds blew and beat against that house; yet it didn't fall, because it had its foundation on the rock. But everyone who hears these words of mine and does not put them into practice is like a foolish man who built his house on sand. The rain came down, the streams rose, and the winds blew and beat against that house, and it fell with a great crash."

If Jesus was here today telling the same story, he would probably say something like this...

Two friends met up and this was the dialogue:

"Hey, Hugo! What's going on?" asked John.

"Hiya, John! What's new with you?" responded Hugo.

"Do you remember that house that I was planning on building? Well I finally found a good foundation, a solid rock, where I can build it. I've worked a long time in building it and soon, once I'm finished, I can move in!" said John.

"Wow!! How great is that!" responded Hugo. "I've also been building a new house. I found a sandy place where it's easy to build. I'll be done building soon and then I'll be able to move in. Yeah, I guess I didn't really take too much time to plan it, but I think it's going to be great!

"Yeah, probably," said John, "I just hope you house can resist the strong winds and rain."

"John, there is one difference between you and I," continued Hugo. "I want to do everything the fastest and easiest way. I mean, my house is practically done. You'll figure it out pretty soon." And he left.

Both men finished building their houses and moved in. Soon the rains came and the winds blew strongly and the waters hit the houses crazily. John's house withstood the strong winds, rain, and floods because he built his house on the rock. But Hugo's house fell.

In His story, Jesus warned those who listened that it was important to love God and build their lives on His teachings. If they didn't, they wouldn't feel secure when they faced difficulties; they would collapse, just like the foolish man's house.

When Jesus finished his story, the people admired the way he taught because he taught with authority, not like scribes.

(Matthew 7)

BIBLE COMMENTARY FOR STUDENTS

Matthew 7:24-29

We all have problems, but Jesus told his followers an important secret. Those who really hear what God says are wiser than those who don't. Many people don't like to do what others order; and when they do what they want, they make mistakes.

On the other hand, we all know that a house needs to have a good foundation so that it remains firm and doesn't fall. Jesus compared people who don't listen to those who build their house on the sand. For a time it will look good, but when the problems arrive, it will fall. He said that people who don't listen to him are making a mistake. He is the foundation, the firm rock.

To those who don't want to listen, maybe for a while everything will be okay. But then the problems will come and they won't be able to resist them. People who obey Jesus also have problems, but they have the courage to do the right thing by listening to the Lord.

In the space below, draw a house built on the rock that is Christ. And another that was not built on Jesus the rock.

Lesson 44

STUDENT WORKBOOK

COMPASSION FOR THE NEEDY

Memory Verse: "Therefore, as we have opportunity, let us do good to all people, especially to those who belong to the family of believers." (Galatians 6:10)

Thousands die from hunger

Driver runs over child and flees

Refugee center needs food, clothes, and toys.

Victims of flood lose everything

Why doesn't anyone do anything?

What is compassion? Use the code to find the meaning of the word "compassion."

T O L O V E   E N O U G H
40 30 24 30 44 10   10 28 30 42 14 16

T O H E L P   S O M E O N E .
40 30 16 10 24 32   38 30 26 10 30 28 10

```
A  B  C  D  E  F  G  H  I  J  K  L  M  N  O  P  Q  R  S  T  U  V  W  X  Y  Z
2  4  6  8  10 12 14 16 18 20 22 24 26 28 30 32 34 36 38 40 42 44 46 48 50 52
```

Showing compassion to the needy

Carefully look at each of the drawings and do what your teacher tells you. Then answer the questions your teacher asks you, and finish the story by writing how you can work together with God to show compassion to someone.

Story 1

There is a student in the class who uses hearing aids to help him hear; he also uses very thick glasses. Some students make fun of him. They say that he sounds weird when he talks.

_____
_____
_____
_____
_____

Story 2

The father of a little neighbor girl lost his job. The little girl has a new baby sister.

Story 3

A old lady lives by herself in the neighborhood. She doesn't come outside often. A nurse visits her house once a week to see how she is doing. Sometimes she sits in front of her house and watches the people pass. Every once in a while she yells at kids that come into her yard.

What can I do for you?

Knock, knock! Elisha hurried over to see who was at the door. He recognized the woman immediately; she was the widow of one of his friends.

"What's going on?" Elisha asked.

"Your servant, my husband, is dead, and you know that he revered the Lord. But now his creditor is coming to take my two boys as his slaves," she said.

Her husband owed a lot of money when he died. The law said that people who were owed money were allowed to take the debtor's family as their slaves, until their work paid for the debt. Elisha knew that the widow had no money. Elisha replied to her, "How can I help you? Tell me, what do you have in your house?"

"Your servant has nothing there at all," she said, "except a little oil."

Elisha said, "Go around and ask all your neighbors for empty jars. Don't ask for just a few. Then go inside and shut the door behind you and your sons. Pour oil into all the jars, and as each is filled, put it to one side."

The widow thought to herself, "What will this little bit of oil do for me now?" But, she closed the door and gathered her sons and told them what Elisha had told her. They went from house to house asking their neighbors for all of the empty jars they could get. Once they were back at their house, the widow asked her sons to please bring her a jar. As they brought the jars to her, she kept pouring. She told them that as each one got full to move it aside so that it didn't get in the way.

The sons saw how many empty jars they had all over the house and said, "How is it possible that with so little oil we could fill all of these?" But they obeyed their mother's instructions anyway. One of the sons passed a jar to his mother and attentively watched how she took what little oil they had and started to fill the empty jar. When it was full of oil, the other son took it away to make room for another jar that his brother brought.

They filled jar after jar. Their mother kept pouring the oil into every empty jar she got. "Bring me another jar." But her son replied, "There aren't any left." Then the oil stopped flowing. She went and told the man of God, and he said, "Go, sell the oil and pay your debts. You and your sons can live on what is left."

Lesson 45 STUDENT WORKBOOK

COMPASSION FOR THE BELIEVERS

Memory Verse: "Therefore, as we have opportunity, let us do good to all people, especially to those who belong to the family of believers." (Galatians 6:10)

Look closely at this picture and circle each person who needs compassion from someone.

Compassion

Who needs compassion?

"One day a woman said to her husband, "I know that this man Elisha who often comes our way is a holy man of God. Let's make a small room on the roof and put a bed and a table in it, as well as a chair and a lamp for him. Then he can stay there whenever he comes to us." The husband paid people to build this room.

"Elisha! Welcome again! Come in, I have a surprise for you!" said the Shunammite woman. She took the prophet to a room she had prepared for him. Elisha had stayed with this family many times.

"Whenever you come to visit Shunem, you are welcome to stay here," she said to Elisha. Elisha thought about the woman and her loving ways towards him, and he wanted to give her something in return. He called his servant Gehazi. "Call the Shunammite. Tell her, 'You have gone to all this trouble for us. Now what can be done for you?'" She replied, "It's okay. I have a home among my own people."

"What can be done for her?" Elisha asked. Gehazi said, "She has no son, and her husband is old." Then Elisha said, "Call her." So he called her, and she stood in the doorway. "About this time next year," Elisha said, "you will hold a son in your arms." The woman had wanted a son, but she thought it would be an impossible thing.

But the woman became pregnant, and the next year about that same time she gave birth to a son, just as Elisha had told her. She was so happy to be a mother! The child grew, and one day he went out to his father, who was with the reapers. He said to his father, "My head hurts! My head hurts!" His father told a servant, "Carry him to his mother." After the servant had lifted him up and carried him to his mother, the boy sat on her lap until noon, and then he died. The mother was inconsolable and went to find Elisha. She went as fast as she could to where he was.

Triple Restitution

Elisha saw her coming from far away and he sent Gehazi to meet her and see if everything was okay, but he didn't say to ask about her son. She wanted to tell Elisha directly, but he gave Gehazi his staff as a symbol of his prophetic authority. "Tuck your cloak into your belt, take my staff in your hand and run. Don't greet anyone you meet, and if anyone greets you, don't answer. Lay my staff on the boy's face."

When they got to the house, Gehazi did as he was told to do and went back to Elisha to tell him that the boy had not woken up.

When Elisha reached the house, there was the boy lying dead on his couch. He went in, shut the door, and prayed to the Lord. Then he laid on the bed beside the boys. As he stretched himself out beside him, the boy's body grew warm. Elisha turned away and walked back and forth in the room and then got on the bed and stretched out beside him once more. The boy sneezed seven times and opened his eyes. Elisha summoned Gehazi and said, "Call the Shunammite." And he did. When she came, he said, "Take your son."

Sometime after, God told Elisha that he was bringing a drought. There would be nothing to eat. Elisha remembered the compassion of the Shunammite woman and went to go warn them. "Get up, take yourself and your household away to live where you can, because God has declared a famine in this land for the next seven years," Elisha told them.

So she and her family left. After seven years, they returned, only to find their home and possessions had been taken. She went to the king to beg for her house and land. The king was talking to Gehazi and he told the king who she was and her story. Once the king heard this, he ordered that all her belongings be returned to her. (2 Kings 4 and 8)

Showing compassion to the people of my church

Memory Verse: "Therefore, as we have opportunity, let us do good to all people, especially to those who belong to the family of believers." (Galatians 6:10)

Look carefully at the drawings on this page and answer the questions that your teacher asks you.

What are the needs that the people of your church have? What can you do to show compassion to them?

Lesson 46 — STUDENT WORKBOOK

COMPASSION FOR THOSE IN AUTHORITY

Memory Verse: "Therefore, as we have opportunity, let us do good to all people, especially to those who belong to the family of believers." (Galatians 6:10)

"Oh no!" cried the young servant girl. "Leprosy? No!" Naaman, her master, had a terrible disease and no one could cure it. She said to her mistress, "if only my master would see the prophet who is in Samaria! He would cure him of his leprosy." Naaman's wife commented to him what the servant had told her.

"Could he really help me?" Naaman asked her. He went to ask the king if he could go to Israel to find this prophet Elisha. The king of Syria said, "By all means, go. I'll send a letter to the king of Israel."

Naaman left towards Israel with his servants, horses and chariots. The letter he took to the king read: "With this letter I am sending my servant Naaman to you so that you may cure him of his leprosy."

As soon as the king of Israel read the letter, he tore his robes and said "Am I God? Can I kill and bring back life? Why does this fellow send someone to me to be cured of his leprosy? See how he is trying to pick a quarrel with me!"

When Elisha, the man of God, heard that the king of Israel had torn his robes, he sent him this message: "Why have you torn your robes? Have the man come to me and he will know that there is a prophet in Israel." So Naaman went with his horses and chariots and stopped at the door of Elisha's house. Elisha sent a messenger to say to him, "Go, wash yourself seven times in the Jordan, and your flesh will be restored and you will be cleansed."

But Naaman went away angry and said, "I thought that he would surely come out to me and stand and call on

ARE YOU JOKING?

the name of the LORD his God, wave his hand over the spot and cure me of my leprosy."

Are not Abana and Pharpar, the rivers of Damascus, better than all the waters of Israel? Couldn't I wash in them and be cleansed?" So he turned and went off in a rage.

Naaman's servants cared for and loved their master and wished that he would be cured. They knew he had already tried everything and nothing had healed him, so they said, "My father, if the prophet had told you to do some great thing, would you not have done it? How much more, then, when he tells you, 'Wash and be cleansed'!"

So Naaman went down and dipped himself in the Jordan River seven times, as the man of God had told him, and his flesh was restored and became clean like that of a young boy.

Then Naaman and all his attendants went back to the man of God. He stood before him and said, "Now I know that there is no God in all the world except in Israel."

Naaman was so excited that Elisha had compassion on him that he tried to give him lots of gifts, but the prophet refused because he wanted Naaman to understand that it wasn't he who had healed him, but God. And that no one can buy favor in the eyes of the Lord.

(2 Kings 5)

What would have happened?

Compassion

for those who have power and authority

Look at each person in the drawings. Think about where they exercise authority, and then answer each of the following questions:

1. Who are the people with power or authority?

2. Why do people with power or authority need us to have compassion toward them?

3. How can we serve compassionately?

Lesson 47 — STUDENT WORKBOOK

COMPASSION FOR OUR ENEMIES

Memory Verse: "Therefore, as we have opportunity, let us do good to all people, especially to those who belong to the family of believers." (Galatians 6:10)

Who in this photo do you think doesn't deserve compassion? The client that is angry at the employee? The man who is stealing the woman's purse? The people on the Wanted! posters?

But, they are the enemy

(A bible story drama)

ACT I

(In a Syrian army camp. A scared soldier enters. You can tell by his face how scared he is. He bows in front of the king.)

Syrian soldier: Your highness! The ambush against Israel has failed again!

Syrian king: (angrily) AGAIN?! There has to be a spy among our men that is communicating our plans to the Israeli king. Go call all of the officers immediately! We'll discover who our spy is!

Syrian soldier: Yes, your majesty! I'll go right away! (He leaves and returns with the officers.)

Syrian king: Will you not tell me which of you is on the side of the king of Israel?

First officer: None of us, my lord the king. Elisha, the prophet who is in Israel, tells the king of Israel the very words you speak in your bedroom.

Second officer: Yes, your majesty! This prophet knows exactly where we are going to attack. His God reveals to him our plans, then he shows them to the king of Israel.

Syrian king: Go, find out where he is so I can send

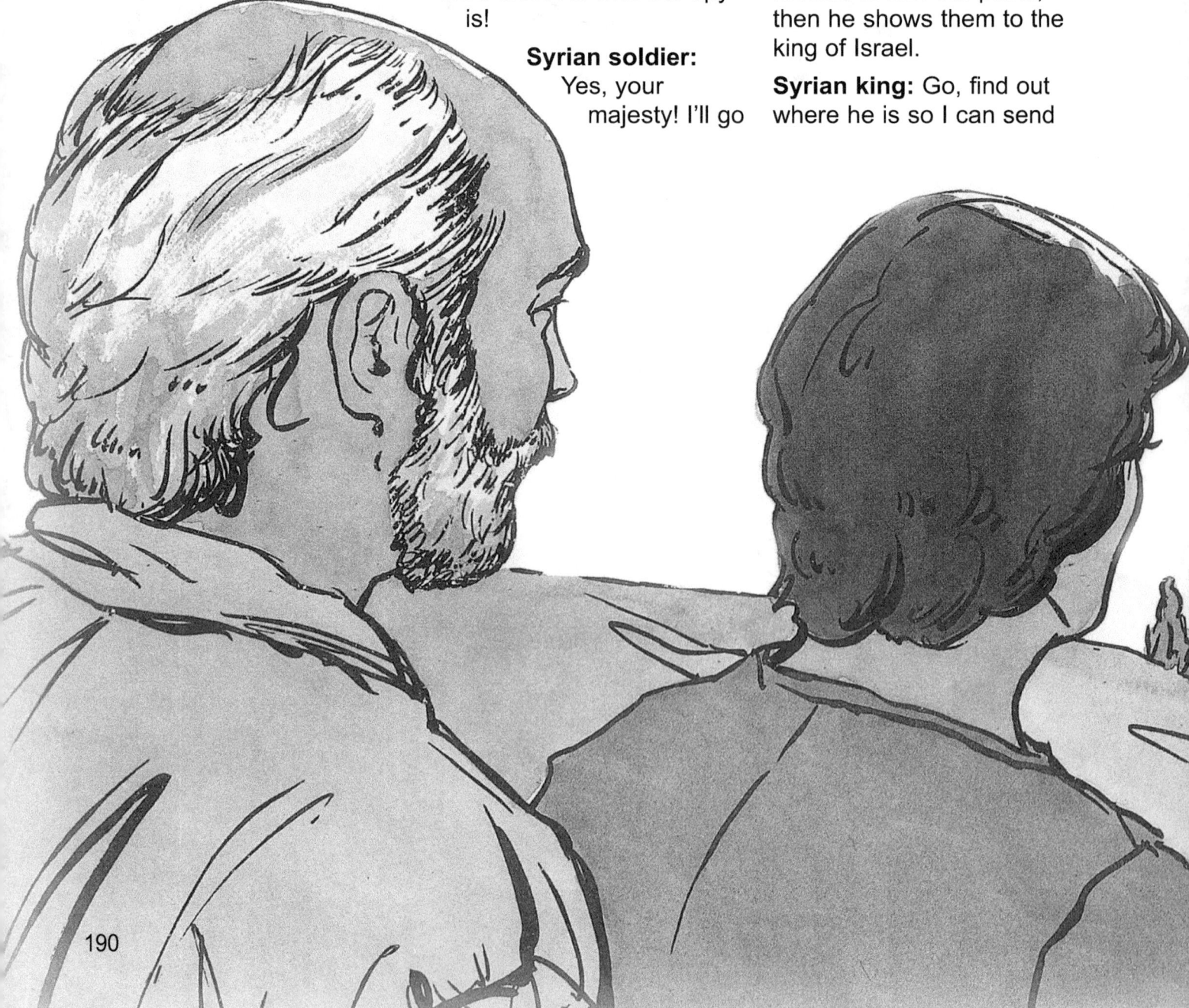

men and capture him.

(The officers leave and the king writes on a piece of parchment. The first officer enters and bows before the king.)

Syrian king: Have you found where the prophet Elisha is?

First officer: Yes, he is in Dothan!

Syrian king: Dothan? Surround the city right now!

First officer: Yes, your majesty! (He leaves.)

Syrian king: (claps his hand together and smiles evilly) Elisha, I'll make you my prisoner soon enough!

ACT II

(Early in the morning in Dothan, Elisha's servant goes to the well to bring in water. He realizes that the entire city is surrounded by the Syrian army. He hurries to tell Elisha.

Elisha's servant: Master, the city is surrounded by the Syrian army! They're going to kill us! Oh my lord, what shall we do?

Elisha: Don't be afraid. Those who are with us are more than those who are with them. (Elisha bows his head and starts to pray.) Oh Lord, open his eyes so that he may see.

Elisha's servant: (looks around him in awe, rubs his eyes) I can't believe what I'm seeing! There are other horses and other chariots on the hills surrounding the Syrians. They are so bright, like they're on fire!

Elisha: (looks to the sky and prays) Strike these people with blindness.

(The Syrian soldiers begin to trip on the road, they have no idea where they're going.)

Elisha: (walks close to the first officer) This is not the road and this is not the city. Follow me and I'll lead you to the man you are looking for.

First officer: (Orders his men) Follow me.

(Elisha guides them to the king of Israel and prays once more.)

Elisha: Oh, Lord, open their eyes so they may see.

First officer: (looks around) Where are we?

Second officer: It looks like Samaria, but it couldn't be!

Israel king: Should we kill them, my lord?

Elisha: Don't kill them. Would you kill men you have captured with your own sword or bow? Set food and water before them so that they may eat and drink and then go back to their master.

First official: Did you hear that? They are going to give us something to eat and then let us leave freely and return home!

Second official: What kind of people are these?

(2 Kings 6)

To the powerful
Write how you can show compassion and mercy to those who have power and authority.

To the needy
Write how you can show compassion and mercy to those who have great needs.

Compassion to the abandoned
Write how you can show compassion and mercy to those who are abandoned and without help.

Write how you can show compassion and mercy to those who wish to hurt you.

Official Badge

My plan of compassion
"Therefore, as we have opportunity, let us do good to all people, especially to those who belong to the family of believers."
(Galatians 6:10)

Lesson 48 – STUDENT WORKBOOK

CHRISTMAS ACCORDING TO THE PATRIARCHS AND THE PROPHETS

Memory Verse: "She will give birth to a son, and you are to give him the name Jesus, because he will save his people from their sins." (Matthew 1:21)

INTERVIEW WITH THE PROPHETS ABOUT CHRISTMAS

Reporter: God has been planning Christmas for a long time. Peter said that Jesus was chosen to come to this world before it was even created (Peter 1:20). After Jesus came, God helped the writers of the New Testament to find the clues in the Old Testament. We're going to talk to one of the most well-known patriarchs and a couple of prophets who personally received hints, or clues from God.

Abraham: Okay, who would have thought? Everything I know is what God told me: "I'll make you into a great nation and I'll bless you; I'll make your name great, and you will be a blessing. I'll bless those who bless you, and whoever curses you I'll curse; and all peoples on earth will be blessed through you" (Genesis 12:2-3).

You guys can imagine how crazy this sounded in the beginning. I mean, my wife and I didn't even have kids! Generations later, out of my family, Jesus was born. He is the Son of God. This is the most amazing thing I could have ever imagined!

Reporter: I can imagine! Thank you, Abraham. My next guest is Isaiah, the prophet. Welcome, Isaiah!

Isaiah: It's incredible to see the way that God

moves and acts. I know of Abraham, I'm one of his descendants. God let his family grow and become many large nations. When I was ministering, the people were always scared that they were going to be destroyed. The Lord inspired me to speak to them about hope. So I told them, "Therefore the Lord himself will give you a sign: The virgin will be with child and will give birth to a son, and will call him Immanuel." (Isaiah 7:14) And he also said: "For to us a child is born, to us a son is given, and the government will be on his shoulders. And he will be called Wonderful Counselor, Mighty God, Everlasting Father, Prince of Peace" (Isaiah 9:6).

Reporter: I've heard of these in stories and Christmas songs.

Isaiah: And you can see why. They describe Jesus perfectly! He came hundreds of years after my time. God used my messages to give hope to his people during this time! If we would turn towards God, He would protect us. But, there's something even better! The Son used my words to help other people recognize that Jesus fulfilled the prophecies in a special way.

And one more thing! He also told the people of Israel about a man who would prepare the way for the coming King. This person would say, "In the desert prepare the way for the Lord; make straight in the wilderness a highway for our God" (Isaiah 40:3).

Reporter: Many years later, Matthew saw that these words described John the Baptist, who prepared the people to hear the message that Jesus carried. Thank you, Isaiah.

My last guest today is the prophet Micah.

Micah: Thank you! It's a pleasure to be here. Isn't it amazing how great God is? Just like Isaiah, I also lived in times of trouble. Israel had divided into two nations. I warned them that their sin would destroy them.

Reporter: How terrible!

Micah: Yes, it was. God was tired of us. But he gave us an opportunity to return to Him. Bethlehem was a tiny town, but important people came out of it, like Naomi, Ruth and even David! I said, "But you, Bethlehem Ephrathah, though you are small among the clans of Judah, out of you will come for me one who will be ruler over Israel, whose origins are form of old, from ancient times" (Micah 5:2).

Reporter: So you were the prophet who gave Herod's men the idea to look for Jesus there!

Micah: All of that happened a long time after my time on earth. But I was the one who prophesied about where Jesus would be born.

Reporter: Incredible! It's no surprise why Matthew and the other New Testament authors were so excited about what they found in the Old Testament. They found the clues that helped people see that Jesus really was the Son of God. His coming to Earth was the last piece of our puzzle.

194

THE SON OF GOD

Baby Jesus was born
In the cold of winter
His bed was not made of flowers,
And he didn't have any pillows
But He is the one who,
lit up the stars in the sky
He showed them how
Through space he'd created to fly

He left all glory behind
Up there in God's special place
He put aside his divinity
wrapped himself up in the human race
He came down to planet Earth
To save the people he loves
Has there ever been such a one,
so noble and pure from above?

All of you who are good;
those who listen anew,
must worship the Child God
because it is our due,
For this reason, I ask you to go,
my kind listeners, I pray
with humble and reverent hearts
go and worship the child God today

—Abraham Fernandez—

Verse of the Month Club

Keep your membership to the Verse of the Month Club going. You can invite a friend from your class to work with you to review the verses until you both have learned them. The texts for this quarter are: Matthew 1:21, John 11:27 and 1 Corinthians 10:31. You'll be so excited when you learn them.

"She will give birth to a son, and you are to give him the name Jesus, because he will save his people from their sins."

Matthew 1:21

"Yes, Lord," she replied, "I believe that you are the Messiah, the Son of God, who is to come into the world."

John 11:27

"So whether you eat or drink or whatever you do, do it all for the glory of God."

1 Cor. 10:31

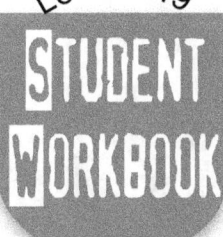

Lesson 49

CHRISTMAS ACCORDING TO ZECHARIAH AND ELIZABETH

Memory Verse: "She will give birth to a son, and you are to give him the name Jesus, because he will save his people from their sins." (Matthew 1:21)

Christmas list

Answer the following questions and write your answers on the blank lines.

What preparations do you and your family make to celebrate Christmas?

_____

_____

_____

What preparations did God make to prepare for the first Christmas?

_____

_____

_____

Preparing the world for the birth of Jesus wasn't all that God had to do. He also had to prepare someone to preach about Jesus. Do you know who did that? The answer is in this riddle:

- My clothes are made of camel skin.

- My belt is made out of animal skin.

- My food consists of locusts and wild honey.

- One of the things I must do is baptize.

"Who am I?"

_____

PREPARATIONS FOR THE SAVIOR

"Is it true that one day we'll have a son?" Elizabeth asked Zechariah.

"I don't know, we are so old already and we've prayed for this for so long," responded Zechariah. Zechariah was a loyal priest who served while Herod was the king of Judea. He and his wife were righteous before God.

One day when it was Zechariah' turn to enter the sanctuary and burn incense, an angel of the Lord appeared to him. Seeing him, Zechariah was startled and scared, but the angel said, "Don't be afraid, Zechariah; your prayer has been heard. Your wife Elizabeth will bear a son, and you are to give him the name John. He will be a joy and delight to you, and many will rejoice because of his birth, for he will be

great in the sight of the Lord. Many of the people of Israel will he bring back to the Lord their God. And he will make ready a people prepared for the Lord."

Zechariah asked the angel: "How can this be? I'm already old and so is my wife"

Responding, the angel said, "I am Gabriel. I stand in the presence of God, and I have been sent to speak to you to tell you this good news. And now you will be silent and not able to speak until the day this happens, because you didn't believe my words, which will come true at their proper time."

"What happened to Zechariah?" people asked.

"He's excited! Look at the way he is moving his arms back and forth like that"

"Actually I think he's trying to tell us something," said someone.

When he had finished his responsibilities at the temple, Zechariah went home with his wife Elizabeth. One day she came home with good news. "Zechariah, we're going to have a child! God has answered our prayers." Six months later, Mary, a relative of Elizabeth's, went to go visit her. When Elizabeth heard Mary enter her home and greet her, the baby leaped in her womb, and Elizabeth was filled with the Holy Spirit. In a loud voice she exclaimed, "Blessed are you among women, and blessed is the child you will bear!"

Mary stayed with Elizabeth for three months. When the time came, Elizabeth gave birth to a baby boy, just like the angel told her. The neighbors and family members celebrated with her.

"What will you call him," they asked her.

"Maybe you should name him Zechariah like his father," suggested the men.

"No! His name is John," said Elizabeth.

The neighbors and family members asked, "Why? There is no one in your family with that name." Then they asked the father what he thought they should name the baby and he asked for a tablet and wrote on it, "His name is John." At that very instant, Zechariah could talk and he blessed God.

John lived in the desert until he appeared publicly to Israel. His clothing was made of camel skin and he had a leather belt and he ate locusts and wild honey. When it was time, he began to preach, "Repent, for the kingdom of heaven is near."

He also said that he was the prophet to whom Isaiah was referring to when he said, "In the desert prepare the way for the Lord; make straight in the wilderness a highway for our God." All of the people from Jerusalem, Judea and from around the Jordan came to hear John preach.

John the Baptist

Look for the Bible verses for each question and write down the answers on the blank lines.

1. Who visited Zechariah in the temple and told him he'd have a son? (Luke 1:11)
   _____

2. What did the angel tell Zechariah he had to name his son? (Luke 1:13)
   _____

3. What name did the people think the baby should have? (Luke 1:59)
   _____

4. Who was John's mother? (Luke 1:13)
   _____

5. What did John eat? (Matthew 3:4)
   _____

6. What did John come to do? (Luke 3:4)
   _____

7. What did John tell the people to do? (Matthew 3:2)
   _____

8. What did John do with water? (Luke 3:16)
   _____

9. What kingdom did John say was near? (Matthew 3:2)
   _____

10. What did John say the One coming after him would baptize them with? (Luke 3:16)
    _____

11. Where did John live? (Luke 1:80)
    _____

12. Which prophet talked about someone coming out of the desert? (Luke 3:4)
    _____

13. With what did John baptize? (Luke 3:16
    _____

Lesson 50 — STUDENT WORKBOOK

CHRISTMAS ACCORDING TO MARY AND JOSEPH

Memory Verse: "She will give birth to a son, and you are to give him the name Jesus, because he will save his people from their sins." (Matthew 1:21)

In the quiet night

Scene 1: Mary and Joseph are talking excitedly.

Mary: Joseph! Something marvelous has happened!

Joseph: What happened?

Mary: An angel came to me and told me, "Greetings, you who are highly favored! The Lord is with you!"

Joseph: And you weren't frightened?

Mary: At the beginning I was, but the angel told me, *"Don't be afraid, Mary, you have found favor with God. You will be with child and give birth to a son, and you are to give him the name Jesus."*

Joseph: Wait just a moment!! You can't be pregnant! We haven't even gotten married yet!

Mary: Yes, I know, but this isn't a normal baby. The angel told me, *"The Holy Spirit will come upon you, and the power of the Most High will overshadow you. So the holy one to be born will be called the Son of God."*

Joseph: (with sadness) But Mary! Did you even stop to think, how could God have a son? I need time to think about this. (Talking to himself) I suppose Mary and I'll have to break off our engagement.

Scene 2: (Joseph is sleeping. The angel appears in his dreams.)

Narrator: Joseph went to sleep, concerned and confused. While he slept, an angel appeared in his dreams.

Angel: *Joseph son of David, don't be afraid to take Mary home as your wife because what is conceived in her is of the Holy Spirit. She will give birth to a son, and you are to give him the name Jesus, because he will save his people from their sins.*

Narrator: All this took place to fulfill what the Lord had said through the prophet: *"The virgin will be with child and will give birth to a son, and they will call him Immanuel"* – which

201

means, "God with us." When Joseph woke up, he did what the angel told him and took Mary as his wife. It was time to pay taxes and the king had ordered that everyone return to the place where he was born to pay and be present for the census.

Joseph: Mary, we need to go to Bethlehem. My family is there. You know that David is my ancestor.

Scene 3: (Mary and Joseph have traveled to Bethlehem. The innkeeper talks to himself.)

Innkeeper: All of Bethlehem is full of people coming to register for the census. The inn is completely full. I hope no one else comes that I have to tell them that I have no more room. Oh…just my luck, another person knocking at the door.

Joseph: Do you have a room available?

Innkeeper: I'm sorry, but the inn is full. You'll have to find another place.

Joseph: We've come from Nazareth. My wife is about to have our baby and she is so tired. You don't have any place where we could rest for a bit?

Innkeeper: I already told you, no! My inn is full. I'd like to help you but…no. Wait a minute. I have an idea. If you want, you can stay in the stable out back. It's all that I can offer you.

Joseph: The stable. Okay, that's fine, thank you.

Scene 4: (Mary and Joseph and the baby are in the corner of the stable. The shepherds have sat down around their campfire when the angels appear.)

Narrator: While they were there, the time came for the baby to be born, and she gave birth to her firstborn, a son. She wrapped him in cloths and placed him in a manger.

In the same region, there was a group of shepherd that were keeping watch on their flocks at night. An angel appeared to them.

Shepherds (scared): What is this? Who are you? Please don't hurt us!

Angel: *Don't be afraid. I bring you good news of great joy that will be for all the people. Today in the town of David a Savior has been born to you, he is Christ the Lord. This will be a sign to you: You will find a baby wrapped in cloths and lying in a manger.*

Narrator: Suddenly a great company of the heavenly host appeared with the angel, praising God and they said:

Angels: *Glory to God in the highest, and on earth peace to men on whom his favor rests.*

Narrator: Then the angels left.

Shepherds: Let's go to Bethlehem and see what the Lord has told us.

Narrator: The went quickly and found Mary and Joseph, and the baby asleep in the manger.

The End

LOOK AT YOURSELF

Jesus didn't become human only for the shepherds of Bethlehem. He was born for you. How do you feel knowing that? Write or draw in the mirror some words of gratitude to God for this. Also remember some happy or sad things that you have experienced this week, and draw it. If you want, you can tell others about your experience.

Verse of the Month Club

Do you need help learning the memory verse? Here is an angel that will help you. Cut it out along the thick lines. Then cut the two horizontal lines that are in the middle of the angel. Now fold the tabs at the top of the verse and insert them where the strips are cut. (If you need help, ask your teacher.)

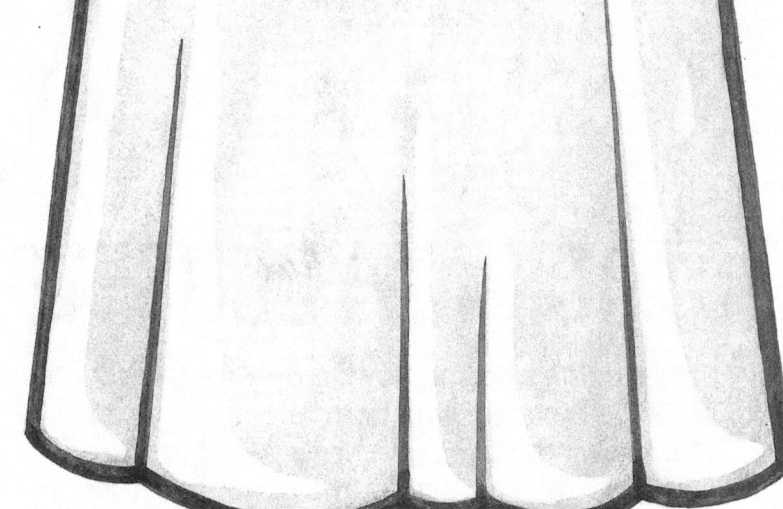

"She will give birth to a son, and you are to give him the name Jesus, because he will save his people from their sins." (Matthew 1:21)

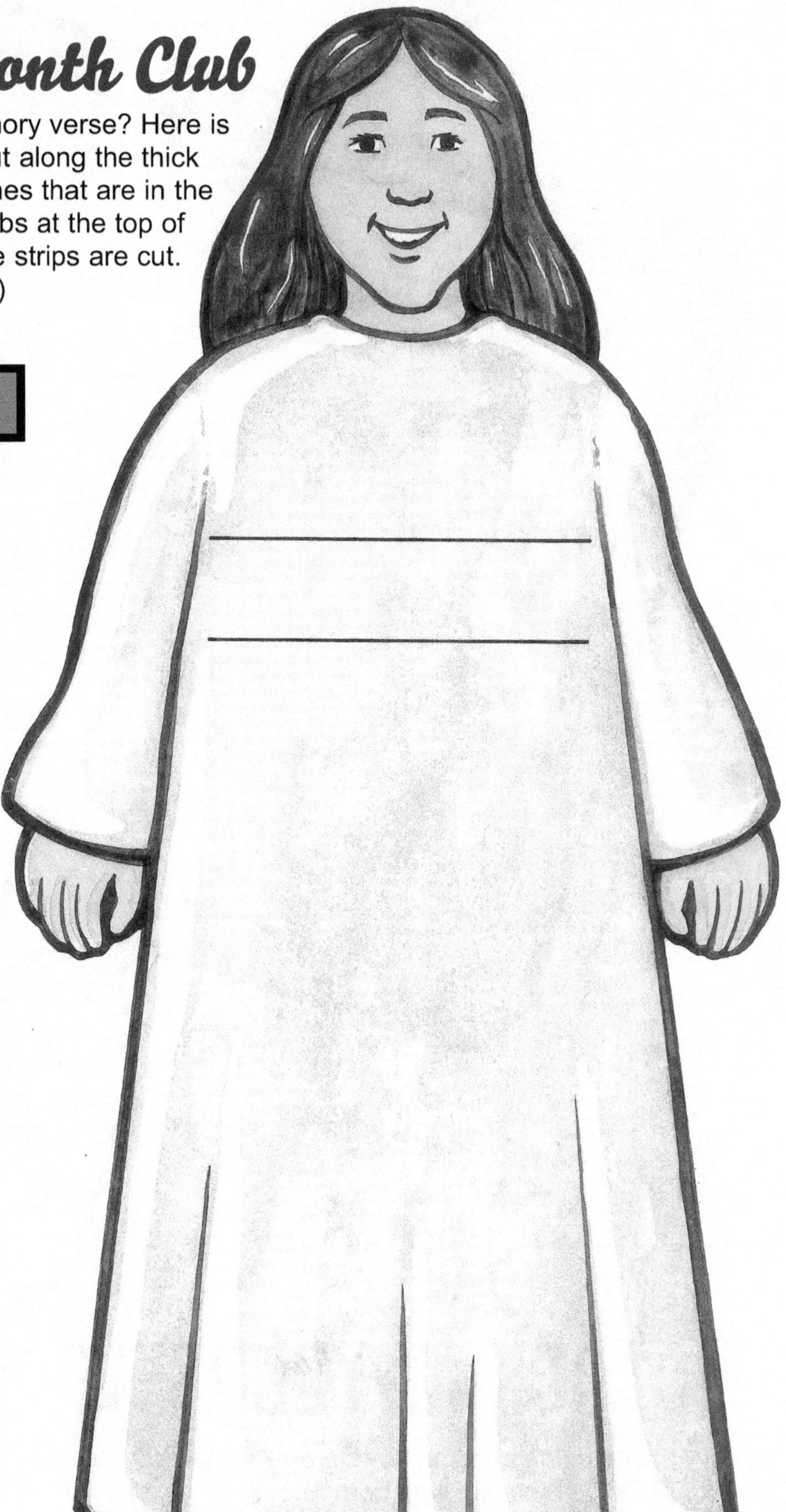

Lesson 51

CHRISTMAS ACCORDING TO SIMEON AND ANNA

Memory Verse: "She will give birth to a son, and you are to give him the name Jesus, because he will save his people from their sins." (Matthew 1:21)

WRITE YOUR OPINION

If a friend tells you that for him, Christmas isn't about the birth of Jesus, but something different as the children on this page say, how would you answer? In the blank space below, write what you would answer to that child about what the meaning of Christmas is for you.

Boy 1
I really like to make and receive gifts, also having big parties. For me that's the real reason why we have Christmas parties. Why put Jesus in this?

Girl
It's okay. Maybe Christmas is Jesus' birthday.

Boy 2
Sure, Jesus was a great person, but how do we really know that he is the Son of God?

A Long-Awaited Welcome

It feels like just yesterday that they were on their way to Bethlehem. Now the baby Jesus already is 40 days old. Joseph and Mary took him to Jerusalem to present him to the Lord. They went on their way to the temple. Now there was a man in Jerusalem called Simeon, who was righteous and devout. It had been revealed to him by the Holy Spirit that he would not die before he had seen the Lord's Christ. Moved by the Spirit, he went into the temple courts. When the parents brought in the child Jesus to do for him what the custom of the Law required, he said, "This baby is unlike any other. This baby is very special because he is the Promised One." He took him in his arms and praised God saying, "Sovereign Lord, as you have promised, you now can dismiss your servant in peace. For my eyes have seen your salvation, which you have prepared in the sight of all people, a light for revelation to the Gentiles and for glory to your people Israel."

Then Simeon blessed them and said to Mary, "This child is destined to cause the falling and rising of many in Israel, and to be a sign that will be spoken against, so that the thoughts of many hearts will be revealed. And a sword will pierce your own soul too. Always remember how special he is."

Anna, the prophetess, was also in the temple that day, she was very old. She never left the temple but worshiped night and day, fasting and praying.

When she saw Mary, Joseph and Jesus, she approached them and recognized Jesus. "This is the baby that we've been waiting for God to send," she said. "Glory to God! Because he has sent the one he promised! I must tell everyone that is near!"

Mary and Joseph were astounded by what she said about Jesus. An angel had come to them and said that he would be called the Son of God. When he was born, some shepherds came from afar and told of a choir of angels announcing his birth and that this was good news for all people. And now Simeon and Anna had recognized the baby as God's chosen one.

When Joseph and Mary had done everything required by the Law of the Lord, they returned to Galilee to their own town of Nazareth.

(Luke 2)

Celebrating Together

Christmas is something to celebrate all year long. Write a list of things that you can do to always celebrate Jesus' birth.

_____
_____
_____
_____
_____
_____
_____
_____
_____
_____
_____

Which items on your list can you tell others? What can you do to help your friends understand why Christians celebrate the birth of Jesus at Christmas? Put an X in front of what you will do during this week to celebrate the birth of Jesus. Get ready so that next week you can tell the rest of your class about your experience of celebrating the joy of Christmas with others.

Lesson 52 — STUDENT WORKBOOK

GIVE EVERYTHING TO GOD

Memory Verse: "For if the willingness is there, the gift is acceptable according to what one has, not according to what he does not have." (2 Corinthians 8:12)

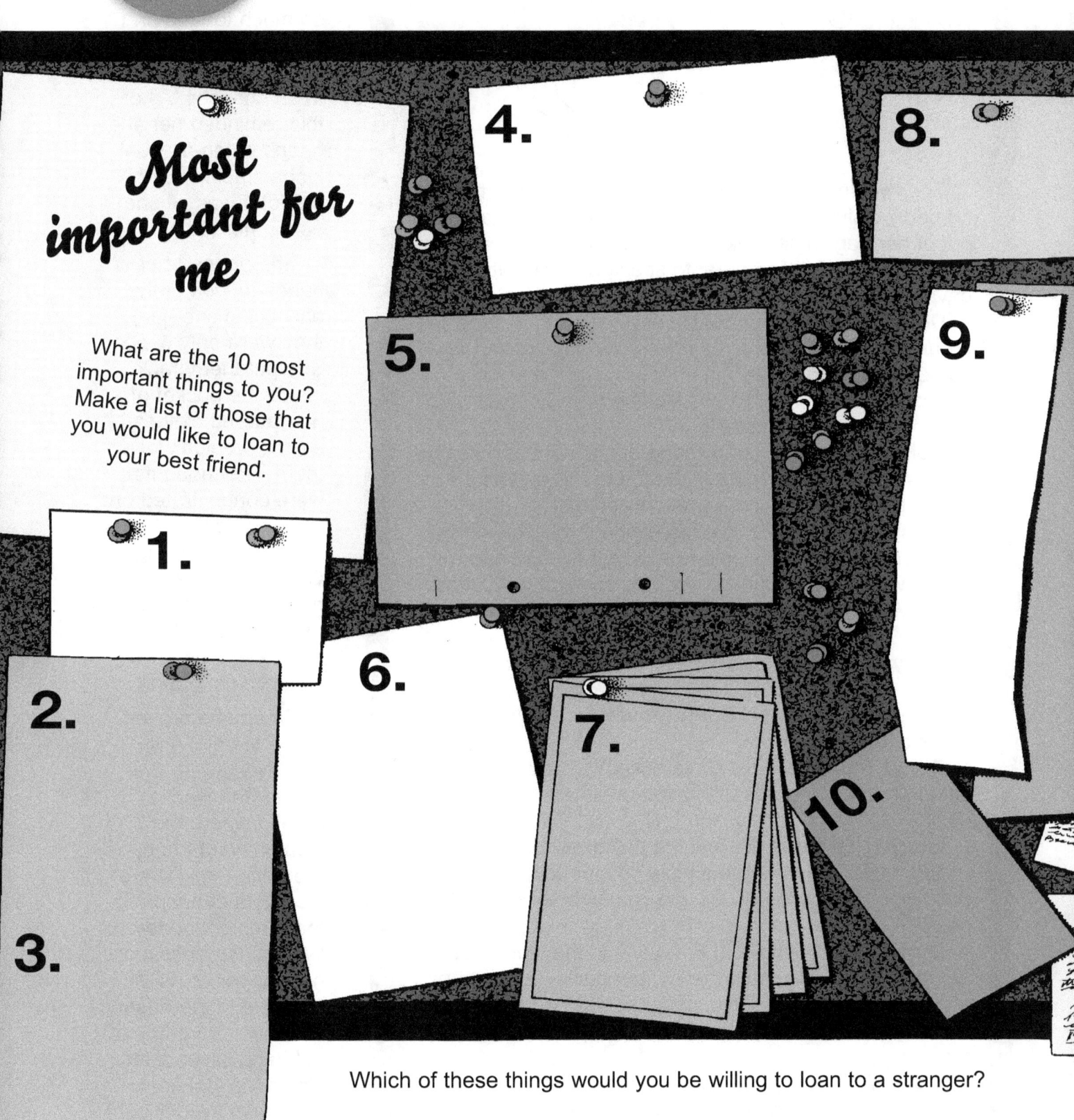

Most important for me

What are the 10 most important things to you? Make a list of those that you would like to loan to your best friend.

1.
2.
3.
4.
5.
6.
7.
8.
9.
10.

Which of these things would you be willing to loan to a stranger?

THE POWERFUL COINS

Part 1

The two small coins belong to a poor widow, who hurriedly walks in the Jerusalem market. She takes them out of her bag while walking. The coins begin to speak:

Mony: Dolly! It's so great to see you again, where have you been?

Dolly: I've been around! I'm always being passed around without stopping. Last week I was even in the purse of a tax collector!

Mony: Seriously? Are you kidding me? Tell me, what kind of coins did you meet?

Dolly: I met some coins made of platinum and some dinaris. Those other coins made fun of me and said I didn't make a difference, I was only copper.

Mony: Yeah, I get it, I've also gone through a similar situation. It's been a couple weeks, but a while ago my owner was a man of power. He had coins of gold in his purse. And you know what? Those gold coins didn't even want to talk to me!

Dolly: It's okay, I guess. Here we are in the market again. I wonder who we'll belong to next.

Mony: Who knows?! But I'm ready for a new adventure!

Dolly: You know what's interesting? This lady that we belong to now, she doesn't have any other coins, only us.

Mony: That's true, it's just the two of us in here.

Dolly: We are only two simple copper coins. She can't buy much with only us. Do you think we're all she has?

Mony: I don't believe it! Everyone in the world has more money than two simple copper coins, but what can someone buy with only two copper coins?

Dolly: Well, look at her clothes, they're ripped and torn.

Mony: And you know what, we are moving a lot. This lady is going really fast! I wonder where we're going!

The coins sit still for a while.

It was late in the afternoon when the lady rushed through the marketplace. She paused every once in a while to look at the food. She wanted so much to stop and enjoy a piece of grape dessert or one of the fresh cheeses. All of this reminded her she hadn't eaten all week, just a small piece of bread! It was all she had in her house.

She opened her hands to look at the only coins she had, they were only copper. She put them back inside the pocket of her tattered clothes so she wouldn't lose them. Her thoughts were concentrated on her small coins. "I wish I had more to bring to God, but this is all I have." She was thankful to the Lord that she even had these two small coins to offer.

When she arrived at the temple, she quickly went up the stairs. She went to a patio where the women went to deposit their offerings. There were lots of people in the temple that day. While she deposited her copper coins, she saw that in the offering box there were lots of gold and silver coins. Her coins looked so small and insignificant in comparison to the

The Widow's Offering

"It could have been" (story found in Mark 12:41-44)

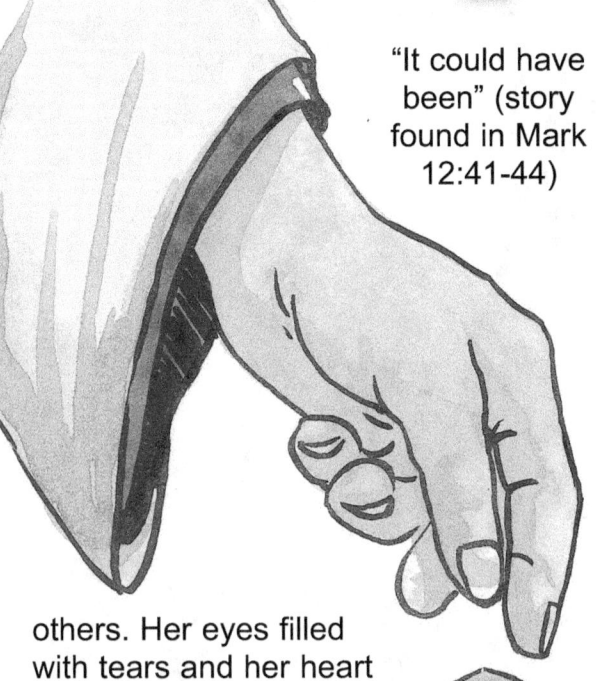

others. Her eyes filled with tears and her heart was content to have brought everything she had to God. After having given her offering, she left the temple.

But, while she was the temple, someone watched everything she did. It was Jesus and he called his disciples and said, *"I tell you the truth, this poor widow has put more into the offering than all the others. They all gave out of their wealth; but she, out of her poverty, put in everything – all she had to live on."*

THE POWERFUL COINS
Part 2

Part 2

The small coins return to the front.

Mony: Did you see where we're at?

Dolly: Yes! We're in the temple offering! It's the first time I've ever been here.

Mony: Me too! I thought we would end up in the marketplace.

Dolly: That lady was really hungry; I imagined we'd stay there too.

Mony: Then, why did she bring us here??

Dolly: (softly) Don't tell anyone but I think we are an offering to God. We were all the money that lady had and she gave us to God. Don't you feel important, Mony?

Mony: Obviously! But I feel uncomfortable being surrounded by all of these silver and gold coins.

Dolly: But, you know what, Mony? There are things that are more important than silver or gold!

Mony: I think you're right!

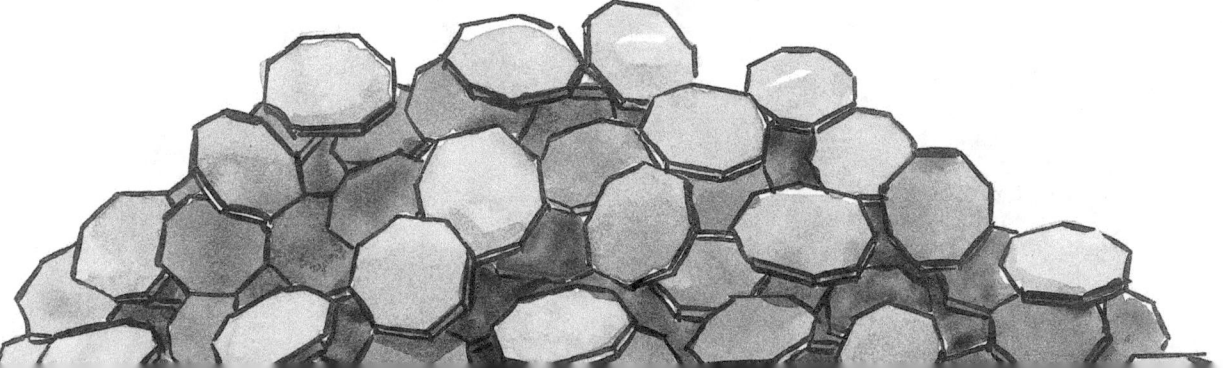

What do you want to give over to God?

If you want to give everything to God, the decisions you make will show that He occupies the first place in your life. What have you decided to give to God today?

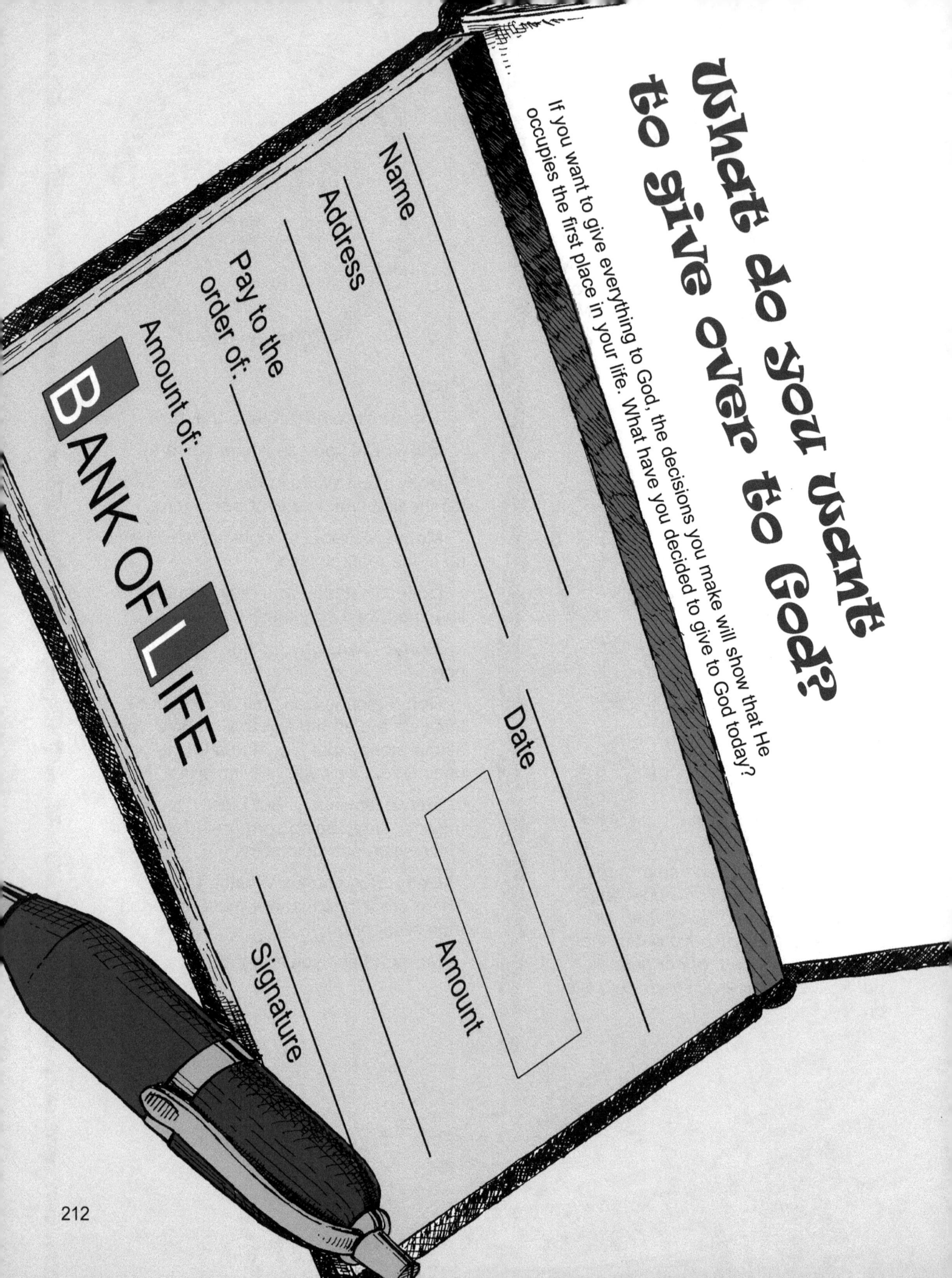

www.ingramcontent.com/pod-product-compliance
Lightning Source LLC
LaVergne TN
LVHW080041090426
835510LV00041B/1869